Boom Town Reflections

Volume – 3

...Into to the Fire

Mark A. Gregg

This book is dedicated to Vangie, the most amazing woman in the world. She is my wife, soulmate, and best friend. We have lived every moment of this incredible journey together. No one knows her fierce tenacity and genuine tenderness like I do.

Table of Contents

~1~
Four Corners

It was the final straw that broke the camel's back! There were other previous events, but when that bullet savagely ripped through the wall of our apartment dangerously close to our 11-month-old baby, we knew it was time to get out of there. *Leaving* the boom town of Rock Springs in 1977 was now my entire life-focus. The irony of this was compelling. My previous life-focus was to *get to* Rock Springs so I could work at the Jim Bridger power plant.

That bullet was the turning point for both Vangie and me. We earnestly began crying out to God to get us out of that miserable hell-hole. Unfortunately, I never gave God a chance to answer. As always, I took things into my own hands and plunged headlong without a clue or a plan. *God obviously protects fools and children.*

It wasn't just the bullet incident. There were ample other reasons to want out of Rock Springs, including Vangie's miscarriage. However, I realized after the bullet incident that my intense, laser focus on working in an electrical generating station put my selfish goals in front of everything else in life, including my family. It was now time to leave Rock Springs, and *nothing was going to stop me!* Unfortunately, I could not see the fallacy of my actions due to immaturity and my own myopic view of life.

I engaged the help of my brother, Larry, who worked for Colorado Ute Electric Association at the Hayden Station in Hayden, Colorado. I impressed him with how dire our situation was and how badly we needed to leave Rock Springs. He then enlisted the help of a man named Harley Kelly whom he worked with for a few years before Harley left Colorado Ute and went to work for Arizona Public Service at the *infamous* Four Corners Power Plant.

Larry phoned Harley and pleaded my case for me. Harley said he was happy to help and could probably arrange an interview for me because the plant was desperate for operators.

Harley agreed to "hand-deliver" a resume' to a gentleman named Kenny McGuire, the Operations Superintendent at Four Corners. I was incredibly thankful for Larry and Harley's help.

A week or so after sending my resume' to Harley, I gave him a call. I was nervous when we finally connected. I needed this man's help, and I didn't even know him.

After several rings, he finally answered the phone. "Hullo?" He sounded like an old man to me.

"Harley, this is Mark Gregg. How are you doing?"

He was breathing heavily as he ploddingly grunted. "Building a *$#@ing fence around my house before the weather gets too cold to finish it, that's how I am doing." He laughed half-heartedly. "It is a pain in the ass. I am building it out of old cement I confiscated from the plant." He chuckled as he said, *"confiscated"*.

I wasn't exactly sure how to read this. I talked to Larry enough to know that Harley drank heavily, was smart, and never let honesty get in his way. I guessed his use of the word "confiscated" could be substituted for ***borrowed without permission.***

3

"I really hate to bother you, but did you give my resume' to the Ops Manager?"

"It's in Kenny's hands." He chuckled. "I know they need operators, but I think they are looking for more experience than you have."

I panicked when he said this. Knowing my experience *was* limited, I knew I had to do something to tip the scales in my favor.

"What if I were to come to the plant when he was there?" I paused to let him mull on this for a moment. "Do you think he would he let me in to talk to him?"

There was an awkward moment of silence before Harley answered me.

"I suppose it couldn't hurt nothing." He answered slowly "It might be worth a try." He chuffed another half-hearted laugh. I was beginning to realize that his laughter attempts were more of a nervous response than a humorous response.

After chuckling, he asked, "You would drive all the way to Farmington, New Mexico, from Rock Springs without an arranged interview?" He paused and laughed again. "Hell, you are *desperate*, aren't you?"

I nervously replied, "I don't think desperate is the right word. I think *determined* is the right word."

"Yup, desperate. Just what I thought." He now openly laughed. I laughed with him. My desperation was obviously showing.

"Tell you what…" His voice trailed off. "You get yourself here, and

I will get you in to see Kenny."

Vangie and I discussed dropping everything, taking a few days off, and going for the interview. She didn't need a lot of convincing due to her intense dislike of Rock Springs.

After talking to Harley and ensuring that Kenny would be at the plant, that next Wednesday morning we packed the car as only Vangie could pack and aimed our red, Ford Pinto station-wagon towards Farmington.

We stopped in Montrose and dropped Brandi, our 15-month-old daughter at Vangie's parents, finishing the journey to Farmington at about 7:00 that evening. We rented an almost squalid motel room, *but it was cheap.* I wanted to see Farmington immediately, but Vangie was tired of being in the car all day, so we just stayed in the motel that evening.

The next morning, I left early for the plant because I didn't want Vangie to sit at the motel longer than necessary. Driving through Farmington for the first time was depressing. The downtown buildings were aging and drab. It may have been nicer than Rock Springs, but not by much. I had to go through a little town called Kirtland before turning off the highway towards the plant.

Kirtland appeared to be firmly ensconced in the "dump" category. The turn-off on Highway 64 onto the plant road had a small, unimpressive sign that said, ***"Now Entering the Navajo Nation."***

In 1978, the Four Corners Power Plant was one of the largest coal-fired plants in the nation. It had five generating units. The first two came on in the early 1960's and were 175 MW each. Unit – 3 was 220 MW and came on in 1964. Units – 4 and 5 were identical 750 MW units.

As I reached Kirtland, you could see the ash billowing from the plant stacks from several miles away. Besides being one of the largest plants in the nation, it was one of the most polluting. Supposedly, the astronauts could see the ash plume from this plant in space.

My heart rate increased with anxiety as I approached the plant. Three of the four stacks belched large amounts of vapor and ash in a violently swirling, white, and gray clash.

I reached the guard gate, pulled into the large, packed parking lot and was greeted by a Navajo Indian man who seemed quite disinterested in greeting me or doing his job. The parking lot was the size of a large ballpark parking lot. I had never seen so many cars parked at one plant, ever.

The round-faced, obese Indian man opened the sliding window in the guard house. It was slightly above the height of the driver's window of an average car. "Who-you-here-to-see?" His speech was halting and careful. He spoke with a strong accent, but it wasn't difficult to understand him. It was more of a problem hearing him due to the steam and equipment noise coming from the adjacent plant.

"Harley Kelly," I hollered over the plant's noise in the background.

The guard took my information and went to his phone. Another car and a truck were now waiting to enter the plant behind me. After a lengthy process of several calls, he came back to the window.

"Park-in-visitor-area-and-wait-for-Kelly-to-come." Another truck and a couple of other cars were now in line behind me. I was glad to no longer be the bottleneck.

It was at least 15 agonizing minutes before Harley came to the guard gate. I had never seen him before, so I didn't know for certain it was Harley. However, I saw the guard pointing him in my direction. He walked confidently towards the car with a wily grin on his face and a swagger of arrogance encompassing him.

He thrust out his right hand and said, "You must be the infamous Mark Gregg, brother of the even more infamous Larry Gregg!" He was smiling like a cat that ate the canary.

"I guess that would be me," I answered, trying to reconcile how he looked to how I thought he should look due to his slow, raspy phone voice. He appeared in his mid-30s, fit, and had short sandy hair and large dark eyes with prominent cheekbones. He looked nothing like I pictured him over the phone. His face looked half-man, half-alley cat with extremely large, dark eyes.

"Come with me. We will go ferret out that rascal Kenny McGuire!"

We walked past unit – 5, then unit – 4, crossing over the huge cooling water intakes and circulating water pumps. We passed several portable trailers and structures to arrive at 'pulverizer alley' on the smaller units.

"This place is a fricking train wreck." He hollered loudly as a safety valve popped and released a deafening belch of steam somewhere in the upper areas between units 4 and 5. I jumped like I was shot. He laughed at my reaction to the safety valve blowing.

We walked into the pulverizer alley on the boiler side of units 3 and

2 to get to the elevator located between units 2 and 1. Even though there may have been ample lighting at one time, the coal dust, grease, and ash were deeply layered everywhere, muting the ample area lighting into a barely visible, dull, yellow hue. The pulverizer area seemed to swallow you in a thick, palatable darkness.

When we reached the area between units 1 and 2, Harley summoned the elevator. The doors opened reticently, revealing a small, filthy, scarred elevator car filled with graffiti and evidence of serious abuse. The elevator car appeared in the same poor shape as everything else I had viewed so far. Harley was the first to talk when the elevator door spastically shuddered closed.

Four Corners Miniature Controls.

"Units 1, 2, and 3 continue to run in spite of the shitty operators here." The elevator bounced and clunked precariously as it ascended to the second floor. As the elevator shuddered and stopped, he grinned broadly, saying, "Units 1, 2, and 3 are about 15 years old, *but they don't look a day over 50.*"

I was filled with awe as we walked from the elevator into the control room for units 1, 2, and 3. The Bridger Plant control room was on the 3rd floor, along with the turbine/generators. The control room here was on the mezzanine deck or the second floor. I thought this was odd. However, it was well-lit and substantially cleaner than anything else I had seen so far.

8

I then saw another completely new thing to me. This control room used miniature controls. The only control boards I knew were the gargantuan Bridger plant control boards. At Bridger, most of the start/stop stations for equipment were large "pistol-grip" hand switches. Here, everything was small, mostly back-lit, pushbuttons. Bridger used large, prominent red and green lights and approximately 4" in diameter ammeters to display the motor current of all the major equipment and electrical systems. Here, they used tiny little meters like a small gas gage in a car. While they had red and green lights indicating stop/start, they were very small. Everything was mashed together tightly to reduce space. All three units were arranged in one small horseshoe area.

Harley abruptly interrupted my train of thought. "Haven't you seen a control room before?" I am pretty sure my mouth was open as I absorbed the ambiance of this control room. I loved control rooms. I loved control rooms far more than I loved stacks.

"Of course!" I answered quickly. "I have just never seen one this small before."

As I continued to be preoccupied with absorbing the sights and sounds of the control room, Harley nudged me to get my attention. "Step into the instrument shop, and I will call Kenny and see if he can see you now."

We shuffled into the instrument shop. He was noticeably suppressing his naturally loud voice as he said, "This plant is union." He looked irritated as he continued. "Therefore, they feel that everyone who works here should be hired at entry level and work their way up. I wouldn't advertise to these guys that you are trying to get hired as an operator."

"Gotcha," I said quietly. "Why are they looking for people with experience?"

"Geez!" He exclaimed loudly. "The government forced APS to hire a gazillion Navajo Indians because we are on the reservation. All the white guys with any experience got pissed and went to other plants. The Indians can't run this place. APS must do something to keep it going." I was completely taken aback by the callous disregard for the Navajos.

After calling Kenny's office, he turned to me and said, "Kenny said to take you to Minnie Bitah, his Navajo secretary. She will give you the standard operator test." He paused and chuckled loudly as he said, "You will probably find the test is a joke, but it's the only thing that the union and management agreed upon to determine if someone is knowledgeable enough to work as an operator here at this plant." My heart skipped a beat. Another test? The problem is, I had not studied for this one.

Entering the "temporary" operations trailer for units 1, 2, and 3 was a shocking mess. There were desks shoved everywhere, and most were cluttered and stacked with papers and tech manuals. There were a couple of younger guys sitting at them, along with Minnie Bitah, a round, middle-aged, angry-looking Navajo woman. Harley told her I was the one who was supposed to take the operator's test. She grunted and told him she would call when I was done.

"Good luck. I will see you in a bit." Harley winked at me with a sly, grossly condescending look on his face as he walked out of the trailer. I wasn't sure if the look was intended for me or against her. Probably both. His disdain for the Navajo people was not guarded.

Minnie cleared a spot by her desk and handed me a two-page

document.

"You-take-test-and-I-grade-when-done." She certainly didn't look very impressed that I was here to take the test.

As Harley said, it didn't take more than a few minutes to realize the test was a joke. I breezed through the ridiculously simple questions. It seemed unbelievable that this was the determining factor in making someone an operator at this facility. I had just finished the second page when a manic, middle-aged man blasted into the trailer. Minnie looked up at him as he trotted past her desk, out of breath.

"Kenny-this-Gregg-Mark-I-give-him-operator-test-do-you-want-talk-to-him?" As with the guard at the front gate, I could understand her, but there wasn't much grammar involved. Kenny stopped abruptly and turned to me.

"Why would want to work here?" He asked incredulously.

"I have family in the area and want to get out of Wyoming." It wasn't a lie. Mom's Dad, Ken Stringer, lived in Bloomfield, New Mexico. It was about 10 miles from Farmington. It flew out of my mouth before I could even think about it. However, it must have worked.

"That's probably the *only* reason I would *ever* move here." He said shaking his head with a look of angst. I was shocked at his response. He was certainly not trying to sell the place to me.

"Minnie," he said quickly, "grade his test and bring it to me when you are done." He quickly disappeared into his office and slammed the door. I could hear him immediately call someone. He sounded angry, but I could tell it was about the plant and not me.

As it turned out, the question about why I wanted to work there was the total 'interview' with Kenny McGuire... *Seriously.* I never saw him again that day. I finished the test and handed it back to Minnie. She immediately called Harley to come and get me. Harley quickly escorted me back to the parking lot, saying he had "a boat-load of work to do".

I drove away from the plant confused, disappointed, and not sure what to tell Vangie. I decided to tell her the interview went well, and I took a test and felt I did well on it. Overall, I would have to mask my disappointment as much as possible.

After retrieving Vangie from the motel, we looked around Farmington for a couple of hours. Our impromptu tour revealed that, like Rock Springs, it did not appear to be a very nice town. However, it did not seem to be overrun with people as much as Rock Springs appeared to be. We then drove to Bloomfield and visited Grandad Stringer. After a short visit with Grandad, we drove back to Montrose as quickly as possible.

We picked up Brandi, visited my folks for an hour, and then returned to Wyoming. We didn't discuss Farmington much because of the uncertainty of it all and the fact that I don't think Vangie cared much more about what she saw in Farmington than she cared for Rock Springs. All I knew was I wanted to work at that nasty, filthy, noisy power station more than I could put into words.

~2~

The Move to Farmington, NM

We were only back in Rock Springs for a few days when Vangie got a phone call from Harley. I was still at the plant getting a little, now rare, overtime. They had a hellish ash spill on unit – 2, and I was staying after class that day to help dig out the bottom ash area.

I called Harley back as soon as I arrived home. He answered the phone immediately. "Harley, Vangie said you called." I was tired but tried to show some energy and assertiveness.

"You did it!" He drolly proclaimed with his expected nervous chuckle. "They are offering you an Auxiliary Operator job. They had a few more of their experienced operators quit, and Kenny said they would offer you a job."

"Wow! That's fantastic!" I exuberantly proclaimed. "When do they want me there?"

"I have no idea. I am just letting you know that Kenny said he would offer you an auxiliary operator's job." This concerned me enough that I knew I had to say something about the almost non-existent interview.

"Harley, he never even interviewed me." I intentionally allowed concern to 'weight' my voice as I continued. "He asked me why I wanted to work there. It seems hard for me to believe this was considered an interview."

"Must have been enough. I am sure they are going to contact you soon." He paused and then slowly, carefully continued. "There is a catch… They are going to offer you an auxiliary operator's job. This is considered semi-skilled, so they won't pay any moving expenses. You will have to move here without any help from APS."

"Doesn't surprise me," I said bluntly. "I didn't expect to be paid to move at this stage of my career." I then lowered my voice so Vangie couldn't hear me. "I just want to get the hell out of here."

About a week after Harley's call, I had still not heard from Four Corners. We had light snow in Rock Springs that day and I was in the little red Ford Pinto station wagon driving downtown to pick up something at the grocery store. As I turned the corner on Century Boulevard near our apartment complex, I apparently hit a patch of black ice. It was as if something were physically pushing the car over the center line instead of turning as I was trying to do.

I frantically tapped the brakes to slow the car down and correct my trajectory, but it wasn't enough. I slid far enough across the center line that I clipped an oncoming garbage truck's massive front bumper in a slow-speed, grinding crash. I wasn't hurt, nor was the garbage truck's front bumper, but the left front fender of the Pinto was demolished. It broke the grill and the headlight, and the fender was folded in, preventing the driver's door from opening. Oddly enough, the wheel and tire were not harmed at all. *The Pinto was still completely drivable.*

When the police arrived, they chastised me for going too fast for the road conditions but let us both go without issuing a citation. The garbage truck had a slight red swipe of paint on the front bumper but no other damage.

I used all my strength to seriously bend and kink the driver's door to get it open, but once I made this "adjustment," it closed and latched with nothing more than a loud creaking sound.

The odd upside to this accident was the Pinto had a sizable loan against it. The credit union loaning us the money required full coverage, low deductible, insurance. We desperately needed moving money to get to Farmington. The $950.00 we later received from the insurance company covered the entire move.

If anyone suggests that I committed insurance fraud, *remember*... I hit a large, five or six-ton, Diesel municipal, garbage truck coming DIRECTLY AT ME! If I wanted to collect insurance money intentionally, I would have picked a much "safer" *stationary* target, such as a tree, instead of a deadly five or six-ton *moving* target.

Besides, I could not have engineered a "better" crash even if I had skillfully calculated and executed a plan with precision. The Pinto looked terribly damaged but was *fully* functional. A few weeks later our insurance company paid $950.00 to repair the damage.

There was a $50.00 deductible, and I simply installed a non-color matching $45.00 fender and grill purchased from a local salvage yard. I netted $855.00 from this crash. Unfortunately, this unexpected income *further* emboldened me to move to Farmington without a formal offer in my hand.

A few days after the car accident, I got Kenny McGuire's phone number from Harley and gave him a call. He was somewhat abrupt and cagey and would not commit to an offer over the phone, but he told me what the position paid. It was $9.55 per hour plus the APS benefit package, which sounded excellent. He stated that human resources would probably be contacting me soon. That was all I needed to hear. As stupid and totally ridiculous as it sounds, I submitted my resignation at Bridger and put together a plan to relocate to Farmington in the coming weeks. Vangie did not realize that I had not received an offer of employment. Had she known I gave my resignation at the Bridger plant without a firm offer, she would have been incensed, and rightfully so.

Joe Johnson and the Bridger people I worked with were quite surprised at my resignation. You see, I really didn't know enough to even be considered an operator, and I had no experience operating anything more than a shovel and an occasional jaunt on a Bobcat. Inexperienced *and* ignorant... Not necessarily the best combination to begin a new job requiring both knowledge and experience. Other than this, I was ready to operate!

The next two weeks were a whirlwind of activity as I patched together the move to Farmington. Joe allowed me to stay in class even though it did not benefit Pacific Power. The class was grinding to completion anyway. I took the rest of my vacation along with a weekend, and we made a second trip to Farmington to find a place to live.

Finding a home in Farmington was far easier than in Rock Springs. We rented a flat-roofed, 3-bedroom, stucco house located at 1037 Zuni Street for less than we were paying for the apartment in Rock Springs. It even had a single-car garage. It was an older home in an older neighborhood in mediocre condition, but it worked well for us.

By the time I completed my two-week notice at the Bridger Plant, I still had not heard a word from Four Corners. I was in agony. I continued executing the moving plan and was now unemployed at

Bridger and still did not officially have a job offer at Four Corners. I couldn't tell Vangie this. She would have a (fully justified) meltdown. I could see her Latina temper explode as she angrily exclaimed, "You did whaaaaat?"

I was truly scared and completely amazed at my stupidity. However, I was committed. We had to go to Farmington. I could see no other option. My alcohol consumption was becoming excessive. I started earlier in the day and drank later in the evening. Vangie hadn't said anything yet, but I knew it was coming.

The weather was now getting quite dicey for moving. It didn't deter me. We loaded the U-Haul truck and put the Pinto behind it using a tow bar. Vangie, Brandi, and I were all in the cab of the U-Haul truck, and we said goodbye to Rock Springs, never looking back.

The weather on the Rock Springs to Montrose trip was not too bad, but once in Montrose we faced a serious winter storm in the 14,000' elevation San Juan Mountains. Winter on Red Mountain pass was daunting, but a 19-year-old driving a loaded U-Haul truck while towing a Ford Pinto station wagon combined with a winter storm on the notorious million-dollar highway in the San Juan mountains was a recipe for complete disaster.

Mom and Dad unfruitfully tried talking me out of leaving. Dad even said he would pay an extra couple of days' rent on the U-Haul if we would wait out the storm. It didn't matter what anyone said. I was of one mind, and that was getting to Farmington even if it was against everyone's better judgment.

As is almost always the case, the snow increased steadily as the altitude increased. By the time we were above Ouray on the million-dollar highway I was questioning my sanity for leaving. There was little traffic because most people had more sense than to be on this road in a storm. It wasn't just the falling snow causing issues; the road was treacherously slick due to a sheet of ice under the falling snow. I was already losing traction causing us to slow down on some of the steeper grades. I knew I had to keep my speed dangerously high to keep forward momentum on the steeper portions of the pass.

The east riverside switchbacks were coming. These dangerous switchbacks are tight, steep u-curves that loop you all the way around. The engineers building the road used them to forge the steep gorges.

Because I was losing traction, I knew the switchbacks were a serious problem. To this day, the first set of switchbacks have a memorial of crosses commemorating lives lost by snowplow drivers and travelers in this area. I was seriously concerned we were going to add to this monument.

Entering the first switchback, the rear wheels on the U-Haul began slipping freely, causing us to slow down. As I gave the truck more power, the engine and wheels sped up, slipping perilously as the truck continued to slow down. Fortunately, we had gained enough speed to carry us through the switchback, but we were now going so fast that I had to 'drift' or slide at a 45° angle through the corners.

I put the truck onto what little shoulder there was because looking in the rear-view mirror revealed the Pinto had swung completely across the other traffic lane. I was fully across both lanes of the narrow, tight curves, sliding the truck around the switchback. Had another vehicle been coming down the pass, there would have been a horrible crash.

It was essential to drift the truck and Pinto across both traffic lanes to get through the switchbacks above Ouray. Thank God there was not any oncoming traffic, or we (and them!) would have been in a real pickle. However, the fun wasn't over yet. What goes up must come down.

We made it to Silverton alive. The worst of the trip was over, or so I thought. We still had to clear Molas and Coal Bank passes. While not nearly as dangerous as Red Mountain and the million-dollar highway, there are still some very steep, treacherous stretches of highway coming out of the mountains.

While descending a particularly steep section of Molas pass, the U-Haul began sliding again. Efforts to slow the rig down were fruitless. Even lightly tapping the brakes caused the wheels to lock and I would lose control of the truck. While trying desperately to reduce our speed, we slid precariously around a corner only to see two stalled vehicles in front of us partially blocking both lanes. I immediately panicked.

"Watch out!" Vangie shrieked as we rapidly approached the two vehicles. I never answered her. I was watching in slow motion what was certain to be a horrible, or even deadly, wreck. The truck was doing at least 45 miles an hour and the road appeared to be blocked. I could not slow the truck down due to the glare ice lubricated by the falling snow on the road.

As we barreled towards the stationary vehicles and certain disaster, I caught sight of a space between them. Initially, due to the falling snow, they appeared to be side by side blocking both lanes. While they did have both lanes blocked, they were not side by side but about 40 or 50 feet apart, each in their own lane. To this moment, I still do not know how we did not clip either or both vehicles. The occupants of the vehicles were standing next to them on the road. Somehow, the U-Haul and Pinto slid perilously between them at approximately 40 MPH as I continued to tap the brakes and slow the truck. I looked directly into one of their terrified eyes as we blew through the perfectly sized opening between them. Somehow, we never touched either vehicle. I still do not know how we missed them.

I wrestled with the truck for several hundred more feet, trying to slow it down after passing them. We never returned as I could not have turned the U-Haul and the Pinto around on a good day, let alone in this storm. To this day, Vangie recounts this event with terror.

God must protect fools and little children. We made it safely to Farmington. We were exhausted, maybe beyond exhausted, but we made it safely. We were able to pick up the key to 1037 Zuni that evening and we "camped" on the floor of the empty house that night.

The next morning, we triumphed over the payload in the U-Haul by getting everything into the house in time to turn the U-Haul truck into the dealer. It was another exhausting day, but we were elated at our progress.

Vangie was now set on making the aging flat-roofed house on Zuni Street our new home. I spent a couple of days helping her make the house livable. I told her I was supposed to start work at the plant next Monday. She still did not know I didn't even have an offer of employment in my hand.

I was terrified to my core and even fretting into sickness at what I may have done to us. We did not have any surplus money, and I had no job offer at this point.

The next several days together at home allowed us to get a substantial amount done at the house. There was not enough money to do much, but we got the utilities transferred to our name and installed a telephone. I was pleased I was able to help Vangie get the house established.

Unfortunately, Monday finally arrived much like a slow-motion, nerve-wracking slide into a diesel-powered wood-chipper. I knew I had to go to the plant for appearance purposes. The reality of my foolishness was now firmly upon me. I was on edge and unable to show it to Vangie for fear that she would call it what it was…*Gross, immature, absolute stupidity.*

While driving to the plant on Monday morning, I decided to play it like I had a job offer. What else could I do? My stomach was in knots, and my intestinal tract was growling and gurgling with reproach as I approached the guard shack. Pulling up to the window, the Navajo guard looked at me with the same disdain as my previous encounter.

"Who-you-here-to-see?" He slowly, laboriously asked.

"Ken McGuire on units 1, 2, and 3." I knew from the previous visit that I had to specify which "side" my contact was on.

"What-your-name?"

"Mark Gregg." He left the window and picked up his phone. I didn't even know if Ken was there today. I hadn't told Harley we were in town because I didn't want him to know I had moved without a job offer. I didn't want him to see the truth…***That I was a total idiot.*** After a few minutes, the guard returned to the window.

"He-say-park-in-visitor-parking-and-come-to-office." I could not believe it. Not only was he there but he also asked me to go into the plant. I parked the car and fearfully walked to the trailer where his office was located. As I entered, I was met by Minnie Bitah, his secretary.

"You-have-seat-and-wait-for-McGuire-not-be-busy." She just stared at me for what seemed like an eternity. I was so uncomfortable I could barely stand it. I waited there, squirming and writhing for almost 40 minutes. I was so nervous I had to make two trips to the restroom.

Occasionally, I could hear Kenny on the phone. Finally, he threw the door open and asked me into his office. *Interesting…* I never even got this courtesy during the so-called "interview."

"What can I do for you, Mr. Gregg?" He seemed just as manic as he was on my previous visit.

"I am here to start work." I looked him straight in the eye and tried to act like I was actually holding an offer of employment in my hand. He was taken aback and stared at me with surprise in his eyes. He then lowered his head a bit, cocking it slightly. A look of total confusion came over him.

"You have an offer from us?" He asked incredulously.

"Yes. I thought I did." I tried to seem completely at ease, but truth be known, I was nauseous and dying right there in my shoes.

"Do you have the offer with you?" He seemed even more incredulous now.

"Oh, I never actually got a **written** offer." I paused, not knowing where to go next. I was now fully in the jaws of the wood-chipper and there appeared to be no salvation. He just stared at me for a moment with a completely confused look on his face.

"Have you moved to this area already?" His voice was rife with amazement and unbelief.

"Yes, sir, I have. We moved into a house on Zuni Street in Farmington." He stared at me for several awkward moments while slowly shaking his head.

"Give me a few minutes to make some phone calls." He pointed to the door. "Go back out and talk to Minnie for a bit... Shut the door behind you."

I did as he said, shutting the door and sitting down at the desk by Minnie. I could hear him on the phone, but it was far too muffled to hear what he was saying. Plus, there was constant activity in the trailer as people circulated through while discussing issues at the plant. Another 20 or so minutes passed. It was chilly in the trailer, and yet I was perspiring. It was truly one of the most uncomfortable moments of my entire life. Finally, Kenny opened the door and looked directly at me.

"Mr. Gregg, I am not sure why you thought you had a job offer, but I need to talk to a few more people. Do you have a phone yet?"

"Yes, sir. We are all settled in." I stated this as buoyantly as possible.

"Well, give your phone number to Minnie, and I will get back to you." He had transitioned from confusion to an air of irritation. I liked the confused look far more than the irritated look.

My spirit was in free fall, and I knew I had a **HUGE** problem. Nonetheless, I stood up quickly and shook his hand, gripping him as hard as possible while looking directly into his eyes.

"Thanks, Mr. McGuire, for handling this. I hope to hear from you soon." I was physically, mentally, and emotionally dying inside and trying not to show any of it. The only outward sign was probably the sweat on my brow. Every pore in my body was pumping perspiration like a porous, water laden sponge.

After giving our new phone number to Minnie, I returned to the little red Pinto wagon and drove out of the parking lot, waving at the Navajo guard as I passed the guard shack. I could not believe what just took place. It was about 10:00 a.m., and I felt like I had just completed 18 hours of exhaustive hard labor. I was nauseous, shaking like a leaf, and feeling as stupid and embarrassed as I had ever felt. *I didn't even like being with me right now.*

Arriving at home, I mustered the energy to continue this facade of sanity and cheerfulness for Vangie. She was surprised to see me at home so soon.

"What are you doing home?" She seemed concerned, and I knew I had to quell this.

"They had a paperwork snafu and had to get human resources in Phoenix involved. They said they would call me when it was straightened out." It was amazing how quickly I could rattle off a blatant lie in those days. She accepted my lie at face value and asked if I would help her hang some pictures. It was then I realized I would live to fight another day even though I was exhausted to my very core. I prayed to God that they would follow through and hire me.

That afternoon and the next morning, I was diligently trying to figure out how I would keep my wife and my sanity when this whole thing fell through as it appeared to be happening. Maybe I could get back on at Bridger? I would have to borrow money from Dad to get us back there if they would even consider rehiring me.

Would Vangie even consider going back to Rock Springs? Every scenario running through my mind just got increasingly convoluted and scary. It seemed the only thing that calmed my mind was alcohol—a fair amount of it. Monday and Tuesday were alcohol saturated. Vangie asked at least twice if something was wrong, but I convinced her I was just nervous about starting a new job. I think she was getting concerned I was not at my new job yet. I didn't want her to realize she was married to an absolute, complete idiot.

Wednesday morning, "THE" phone call came. I had not been far away from a drink *or* the phone since Monday.

I snapped the phone up and quickly said, "Hello."

"Could I speak to Mark Gregg?" The caller was a man with a very pleasant voice.

"Speaking."

"Mark, this is Jim Sellman. I am the Lead Shift Supervisor at Four Corners on units 1, 2, and 3."

"Nice to meet you, Jim." My voice was shaking, and I could not calm it.

"Ken McGuire asked me to follow up on your employment here at the plant." He paused for a moment. "I called your previous supervisor, Joe Johnson. You had him listed as a reference."

"Yes, sir. He was my supervisor and my instructor at Jim Bridger Plant." Jim laughed lightly.

"He indicated that you were the greatest thing since sliced bread." Upon hearing this, I exhaled loudly and hoped Jim did not hear it. "Anyway, we don't have a clue where the mix-up occurred about you being hired here, but we are going to extend you an offer. You should be hearing from Valerie Jordan today. She is our human resource lady here at the plant."

I was light-headed and overwhelmed as I answered, "I appreciate that. I am sure sorry for any confusion this caused." The release of emotion had me fighting back tears and I was shaking almost uncontrollably.

"No problem. Just wait for Valerie to call, and she will get you on board. I look forward to meeting you in person."

I thanked him and hung up the phone. Shaken to my core, I was thankful beyond imagination about not having to face Vangie and tell her I wrecked our lives and ruined any chance I had of working in an industry that I so loved. I immediately thanked God for the phone call.

It only took an hour or so for Valerie to call. She explained I needed to sign an offer of employment and attend the new-employee orientation. I was supposed to return to the plant Friday morning at 10:00 to take care of all the human resource issues. When this was complete, she would provide me with a starting date… *Probably Monday.*

I could hardly wait for Friday morning. It would be the very first time I went to the plant feeling excited about my new job and not nervous about a non-existent interview or terrified about a non-existent job offer. I decided to call Harley Kelly and tell him that we moved to Farmington.

~3~

Unstable Coal Flow

Friday morning came quickly. I went to the plant and sat through the new employee orientation with a couple of other people working in

Four Corners Plant (After the Turbine Decks were Covered)

different areas. I was the only operations person there. The other two were maintenance personnel. The human resources hack explained the extensive Arizona Public Service benefits package and answered all our

28

questions about paydays, holidays, shift work, and retirement. I was quite impressed with APS. Their pay scale was close but not quite as high as Bridger's, but they had excellent benefits. I was being paid $9.55 per hour and based on what Valerie said, there was tons of overtime in the operations department due to "manpower shortages".

I signed the official offer letter, and she made me a copy of it. I was supposed to start at 7:00 Monday morning. I would be on day shift for a few weeks for training purposes and then assigned to a shift.

Driving home from the new employee orientation, I could not help but pray out loud and thank God they hired me. The thought of this going the other way still sent chills down my back. What I did was incredibly stupid and immature. However, I dodged one of the biggest bullets of my life. Again, God must protect fools and children. I was pretty much both.

Harley and Loren Kelly invited us over to their house for dinner that Saturday evening. Even though we were about broke, I insisted we buy a record album as a gift for Harley to thank him for all the help he provided me in getting the job at Four Corners.

Against Vangie's objections, I purchased Boston's first self-titled album. Boston was a rock group in the mid to late 70's that became enormously popular with hits like "***More Than a Feeling***" and "***Long Time.***" The album was a huge hit in the late 70's as well as that night at Harley and Loren's house.

Harley was a heavy drinker. He could down a serious amount of liquor. After Loren put their kids to bed and Brandi was asleep on their couch, Harley broke out some marijuana and a large water pipe. I was already quite inebriated, enough so that I did not particularly notice Vangie's irritation.

Apparently, the large jug with wine would temper the pungent odor and taste of the cannabis smoke as it bubbled through the wine in the jug. I took a couple of large "hits" off one of the tubes from the jug. I was already so drunk I honestly don't recall feeling anything but being drunk. Whatever effect the pot had on me was muted by the excess alcohol in my system.

It was not long after the water pipe was put into use that Vangie insisted we go home. There was no protest because I was in no shape to drive. I didn't realize when we left that she was angry over the serious amount I drank that evening, as well as my willingness to smoke pot with Harley.

The next morning, I was in hangover hell. Plus, I had to deal with Vangie's coldness. One was as unpleasant as the other. She was still irritated over the activities of the previous evening. The hangover slowly subsided that day. Unfortunately, Vangie's anger didn't. She was mad at me the entire day. She didn't appreciate how much I drank and the fact that I smoked (pot) with Harley. I didn't let it get me down because I was so excited about starting my new job Monday morning at the plant. It was all I could think about. I avoided Vangie as much as possible that Sunday.

I arrived early at the plant Monday morning. I was primed and ready for action. It felt wonderful to enter the plant through the *employee* gate. During my orientation Valerie instructed me to report directly to Ken McAdam's office on Monday morning. As it turned out I interrupted a meeting when I entered Ken's office trailer. Several people were sitting helter-skelter in the open area and Ken McGuire was talking. As I walked in, he immediately addressed me in an irritated voice.

"Gentlemen, this is Mark Gregg. He is a new Auxiliary Operator here at the plant." With little pause or fanfare, he looked directly at me and continued. "Mark, just head upstairs to the control room, and I will let the Shift Supervisor know you are here."

I left the trailer excited about going to the control room. I used the steps on the front of the plant, entering the control room from the front side. A diminutive, gaunt, bald 40 + year-old man stood in front of the unit – 1 control board looking extremely stressed out. The unit–1 control board flashed numerous alarms with the associated ringing bells. He never paid any attention as I stood watching him. He was intermittently on the plant paging system with a plant operator. His voice was high-pitched and urgent.

"I got unstable coal flow on 1 B mill!" He was frantically pushing a button on the control board. "I can't get the ignitors in… Go to the burner front and see if there is a problem with the gas guns." He repeated this a couple of times to whomever was on the other end of the phone.

After it appeared things were settling down, I decided this would be a good time to address him.

"My name is Mark Gregg. I was just hired as an auxiliary operator." He quickly turned and looked directly at me.

"Why?" His response was terse and obviously sarcastic. I wasn't quite sure how to answer him.

"Why is my name Mark Gregg, or why was I just hired here?"

"Neither… *Why the *$#@ would you come here*?" The alarm bells started ringing again, and he immediately jumped on the paging system and began to yell. His voice jumped an octave.

"*The ignitors tripped on B mill again! The igniters tripped on B mill again!*" I could hear his pleas echoing on the PA system out in the plant. His voice dropped as he banged on the buttons in the middle of the control board.

"Sorry, my name is Jim McMaster. I've only been here a few months myself." He didn't even look at me as we spoke, so I never bothered to try and shake his hand. He angrily continued. "This place is a joke. You should have stayed where you came from…. *BURNER B-2! BURNER B-2!*" He frantically screamed again in the paging system as he looked between the control board and the alarm panel.

While he was fighting his battle on the unit–1 control board, I noticed some alarms coming in on the unit–3 control board. I stepped closer to it and looked at the flashing alarm windows. As I began to read some of the flashing alarm windows, there was a dull, quick thud, and a ton more alarms began to sound. The main steam master in the top center of the control board quickly went over to the peg reading + 250 psig. In the distance, I could hear the roar of safety valves blowing on the boiler.

I realized the unit – 3 steam-turbine, tripped off-line. When the steam turbine trips, all the steam inlet valves slam instantly closed to immediately stop steam admission into the turbine. This prevents horsepower from entering the generator allowing it to safely disconnect (trip) from the power grid. However, it appeared to me that the coal pulverizers were still running and there were still fires burning in the boiler. There were red lights on the coal pulverizers (red is running in the power industry, green is stopped), and the flame scanners or "fire-eyes" electronically indicated that flames were *still* burning in the boiler.

Large steam power plants deal with a tremendous amount of stored energy. Unit–3 turbine, when at full load, developed over 300,000 horsepower.

"Jim, I think unit – 3 turbine just tripped, but the fires are still 'in' on the boiler!" He spastically reeled around and looked at the control board.

"***Don't just stand there, trip the damn fires!***" I was shocked that he asked this. I have been in this plant for under 30 minutes, and he wanted me to do something on the control board. At that exact moment, a razzed-looking 'maniac' came racing around the corner of the unit – 3 control board. He apparently hooked his foot on the corner of the panel and went persuasively to the tiled floor with a loud gasp.

I studied the control board enough to see three red, shrouded buttons that tripped each of the three pulverizers. I pushed them, and it appeared the fires then tripped from the boiler. An alarm stating BOILER MASTER FUEL TRIP started flashing along with a couple of dozen other alarms already flashing.

Alan Carney, the Shift Supervisor, was the frantic man who had just kissed the deck. He would later become my supervisor, with Jim McMaster as my Control Room Operator. Carney quickly scrambled to his feet, looking disheveled and panicked.

"What's going on? It sounded like one of the units tripped!" he gasped, breathless and visibly pale. Jim remained silent for a moment, so I stepped in and answered as best as I could.

"I think the turbine tripped, and the fires didn't go out." I pointed to the control board and continued. "I stopped the pulverizers, and the boiler appears to be tripped now." He then looked directly at me with the wild look of a caged animal in his eyes.

"*Who the hell are you?*" I could discern a Southern accent. I found out later while car-pooling with him that 6 months earlier he was working at the gas-fired Decker Creek Plant in Texas before coming to Four Corners. He had about 3 years of total experience in power plants but was able to get hired here as a shift supervisor even though he had absolutely no coal-fired experience prior to coming to this plant. During the late 70's, this was unheard of in the industry. Shift Supervisor's usually had at least 10 years or more experience.

"My name is Mark Gregg. I am the new Auxiliary Operator." He turned and ran back to his office and grabbed a hard hat.

"*Follow me! We must get rid of some pressure on the unit–3 boiler!*" He then raced out the front door of the control room and up the stairs onto the turbine deck. I was on his heels the entire way. We ran past the unit–3 turbine that was now rolling down and then over to the unit – 3 boiler drain stand. This is a group of 8 or 10 drain valves for the superheaters and reheaters on the boiler. One of them was the division wall drain. It is a high-temperature superheater drain before the steam goes to the turbine.

"GET THESE DRAINS OPEN NOW!" He screamed at me over the overwhelming roar of the safety valves blowing on top of the unit–3 boiler. *"WE MUST GET SOME PRESSURE OFF THIS THING!"*

It is critical to understand how utterly stupid our actions were. I killed the fires in the boiler before we ever left the control room. This means that there was no more energy being added to the boiler. The boiler safety valves were working as designed by opening to relieve the excessive steam pressure to the atmosphere. We should have remained in the control room to ensure the turbine and related systems shut down properly and not run wildly into the plant as we did.

The first valve I quickly spun open was the drain on the division wall superheater. It is the highest-temperature superheater in the boiler and is located right before the steam goes to the turbine. This drain line is routed under the boiler to a large tank called the continuous blowdown tank. It is a quenching tank that vents to the atmosphere. The drain line was located inside a large, grating-covered trench that goes under the bottom-ash hoppers. From years and years of dumping the bottom ash on the floor due to plugs in the ash removal system, this trench was almost perpetually filled with heavy, wet ash.

Unfortunately, the division wall drain line sat buried in this continuously wet, abrasive environment for years. Normally, these drain valves and the associated piping are only used when the boiler has minimal pressure and temperature. Spinning this valve open during an over-pressure situation with it being severely compromised by rust and corrosion caused it to instantly split wide-open, plus it was currently covered with thick, chunky bottom ash.

The resulting steam release when this 2" line ripped open blew scads of bottom ash over most of the plant. It was raining down small, medium, and large rocky debris much like a Kansas hailstorm prior to a tornado. Besides being severely pelted with ash falling from the sky, the split drain line provided strong competition with the safety relief valves on top of the boiler for the most deafening noise. Frankly, it was terrifying. It was a very good thing that this was an outdoor unit or the amount of steam blowing from this drain could have displaced the oxygen in the building.

Alan spun around on his heels and took off in a dead run across the turbine deck without saying a word. Not knowing what the heck was happening, I readily followed him. We ran across the turbine deck and down the stairs into the control room. He grabbed the phone on the control room operator's desk and dialed Ken McAdam's phone number. Ken apparently picked right up. Sounding much like a six-year-old schoolgirl, Alan hollered into the phone, "Kenny, Kenny, something really bad happened, and it wasn't my fault!" I couldn't believe he just said this. I was young, immature, and an occasional prolific liar, but I knew this was just plain wrong.

There you have it… *My first hour as an Auxiliary Operator at the infamous Four Corners Power Plant.* No matter how crazy it sounds, it is exactly what happened that morning. A sane response would have been to walk away right then, but I didn't. Unfortunately, this was the first of many crazy events that shaped my tenure at Four Corners. Heck, many of the things that happened at Four Corners shaped my life.

The remainder of the day was a blur. Alan had me follow another auxiliary operator around as we attempted to restart unit – 3. I don't know if they ever figured out what caused the turbine to trip or why the boiler *didn't*. Ironically, for training purposes, I was following another auxiliary operator who I am sure did not know much more than I did. *It was indeed the blind leading the blind.*

~4~
Could It Get Worse?

It was not long before I was putting in substantial overtime hours. Having never actually been an actual operator, my learning curve was staggeringly vertical, and I was struggling. It was only a few weeks before I was taken off straight day shifts and assigned to Alan Carney's shift.

I never worked shift work prior to this even though I lied and told everyone I had. It was an extreme shock to my system to go on the graveyard shift (11:00 PM to 7:00 AM). It turns out my circadian clock did not appreciate night shifts, leaving me unable to sleep during the day and unable to stay awake during the night.

In those days, power plants almost exclusively used 8-hour shifts. It wasn't until several years later they changed to the much more popular 12-hour shifts. They were more popular because of the long stretches of time-off each month, and you were never on a shift for more than four days. The 8-hour shift schedule used at Four Corners would put you on the graveyard shift for 7 straight nights. It was a heinous punishment for people not fortunate enough to deserve day shifts.

On one particularly bad graveyard shift I was checking equipment in the plant basement. I was bathed in the warmth of the running plant and fully engulfed in the rhythmic din of the plant equipment. I fell asleep while walking and ambled right into the side of the unit – 2 condenser, immediately dropping me to the floor. It hurt. I couldn't believe how difficult it was to stay awake. Yet, arriving home that morning, I could not sleep. It was terrible. It was cruel and unusual punishment for undiscovered crimes against humanity.

I never dreamed I would loathe shiftwork as badly as I did. I loved the job but hated the graveyard shifts. However, I was still fixated on the goal of becoming a control room operator. My scant taste of it on the first day left me wanting more.

Farmington and the Navajo issues in that area of New Mexico was quite appalling. The level of alcoholism and substance abuse was far beyond what most people knew. We only lived there a short time when we almost ran over a man who was sprawled prostrate in the road, in front of the local post office. Rain was pouring down in sheets as it often can in the southwest. Vangie and I were driving downtown when I saw something on the road. At the last minute, I realized it was a man! I swerved, pulled over, and ran to him.

It was an approximately 50-year-old Navajo Indian man laying right in the lane of traffic. He was big in stature and big in his belly. It took all my strength to drag him to the curb. He was alive but only semi-conscious. He wreaked of alcohol and a ton of other prominently foul smells.

After pulling him to the curb, I ran inside the Post Office and used the payphone to call the police. I was quite rattled and very concerned for this poor man. It took them about 20 minutes to arrive. I stayed out by the old guy, making sure he was okay. He became agitated prior to the police arriving, so Vangie and I were doing our best to comfort him.

Upon arriving, the police immediately lifted him up and slapped him around a little bit. I could not believe my eyes. They then began the arduous task of loading him into the back of the patrol car versus an ambulance, as I thought was needed. He vomited halfway into the patrol car. They let him drop back to the road and kicked him a couple of times. If I had not seen it I would not have believed it. It was obvious now that he was just completely drunk and even more obvious that the cops didn't have any patience for drunk Navajos. They finally forced his semi-conscious body back into the police car, wallowing in his own waste. It was a pathetic and scary sight that burned indelibly in our minds forever.

Vangie and I continuously read about the numerous issues with the Indians in the local newspaper along with the constant call for foster parents. A few months later we decided we would become foster parents. We expected a major process to 'qualify' for foster parenting. It turns out all they really needed was 'unplanned baby-sitting services' but deemed it "foster parenting."

Many Navajos would hit the local bars in the evenings. It didn't matter whether it was hot, cold, raining, or whatever the weather offered that day. Some would leave their kids, sometimes babies, in the car. This could be for 30 minutes or 3 days. The police would make the rounds of the bar parking lots, collect the kids, and deposit them with "foster parents." This could be for a day or a week.

Our experience was that the kids would be reunited with their parents in less than 3 days. Again, this was not foster parenting. This was babysitting. It was heartbreaking, and it didn't take long to realize we could not make a difference. The kids, for the most part, were hardened to it, and the system appeared to be forever broken, locked into this repetitive pattern. We simply didn't have the heart for it and bowed out.

Ironically, I was boozing extremely heavy now. It helped me sleep on shift work. Great excuse, right? Working as an operator was good and bad. I realized the six-month training class at Bridger was entirely inadequate for what I was doing. Because of this, I was getting a well-deserved reputation for being a bad operator. Okay, I was getting a well-deserved reputation for being a **terrible** operator. Two plant mechanics witnessed my first huge mistake not long after going on shift.

The steam drum on the unit − 2 boiler is approximately 6' in diameter and 50 or more feet long. The steam drum is the interface between steam and water in the boiler. The steam generation tubes from the furnace area are attached to the bottom of the drum. This steam water mixture comes into the drum and passes through centrifugal separators. Everything that has enough energy to make it through the separators leaves the top of the drum as saturated steam and goes to several superheaters.

Boiler code requirements during those days stated there must be at least three drum-level monitoring devices on the steam drum. Failure to maintain adequate level in the drum would cause the steam generation tubes to starve for water, overheat, and fail. This, of course, is a safety hazard and shuts the plant down for expensive repairs. *These monitoring devices included a mandatory high-temperature, high-pressure external sight-glass assembly.*

Because the pressure at the drum could be more than 2800 psig, and the temperature would be 650° or more (depending on the pressure), these sight glasses were extremely expensive and finicky. Once leaking, they must be isolated, removed, repaired (at substantial expense), and reinstalled. When they were reinstalled, ***they had to be warmed-up very, very slowly and carefully if the unit was running.***

I was tasked with removing the "hold" tags, or safety tags, and putting a brand-new sight glass back in service on unit – 2. Two plant mechanics were required to accompany me when the clearance or hold tags were removed. Once the tags were officially removed, I was supposed to put the sight glass in service. No problem, right?

While the two mechanics observed, I carelessly and quickly spun the steam-side valve open without so much as a thought about slamming the cold sight-glass with super high temperature steam. When the 500°+ steam slammed the glass, it instantly disintegrated before God, me, and the mechanics.

Fortunately, it was equipped with an internally seating safety blowout ball that closes on excessive flow. Because of this, no one was injured but the new sight-glass was destroyed in the blink of an eye as the mechanics looked on. I could not even lie my way out of it. They just looked at each other, shook their heads in total disgust, and left.

I closed the steam valve to the remains of the sight-glass and returned to the control room in shame. My indiscretion circulated through the plant faster than light. The sarcastic comments and thumbs-ups from people I didn't even know started becoming routine. It was humiliating beyond imagination.

Not many days after the sight-glass event, I worked overtime during a start-up. One of the best control room operators in the plant sent me to the fuel gas system to open a block valve. I had not studied this system yet. I opened what I thought was the gas block valve to the ignitor system. Turns out it was the main vent valve. Large quantities of natural gas vented to the atmosphere for over an hour while they were trying to figure out why they could not get the ignitors in service. The line vented on the top of the boiler, so I could not see or hear it from the area of the valve I opened.

When the Shift Supervisor and other operators finally figured out why they could not get the ignitors to start, they corrected my mistake and told the control room operator what I did. Several minutes after it was announced on the paging system that they finally had the ignitors lit in the boiler, I walked into the control room to see what they found. immediately, the best control room operator in the plant spun away from the control board and, putting his bony finger square in my face with unrestrained rage, screamed at me.

"YOU! Don't you ever, ever, ever touch ANYTHING on my shift again! Don't do anything! Go hide somewhere and sleep, or just leave. We are better off without you!"

As he finished his rant, the Shift Supervisor ran out of his office to see what the commotion was and told the operator to back off. Didn't matter. The damage was fully done. I was embarrassed, humiliated, crushed, defeated, despondent, and more determined than ever to improve my job performance.

I later surmised that the first responsibility of an operator must include a complete understanding of the piping systems. Power plants are almost nothing but piping and valves connecting all the systems and equipment together. I immediately started studying the piping prints, learning every inch of piping and the valves. My reputation as an operator was total, complete crap now. I honestly had nowhere to go but up. Don't get me wrong. I was still immature and making poor decisions. However, I was trying to take steps to at least have a *clue* what was happening in the plant.

Sadly, I was not the only person making questionable decisions. Due to the rapid, unrestrained turnover in the plant, they sent Bob Arnold, a Shift Supervisor of dubious technical ability, to Detroit Edison to recruit "new blood" for the plant. Bob was a decent person but a terrible Shift Supervisor.

During his recruiting trips back east, he would park by a plant's front gate and flag people down as they departed from some of the larger plants, asking if they had an interest in moving to the sunny southwest. Unfortunately, *he was successful.*

Bob convinced several people with 20 + years of experience to come to Four Corners to be Shift Supervisors and Control Room Operators. Most of them had only been Auxiliary Operators due to minimal turnover in their plants. Therefore, APS was putting men with many years of experience doing only entry-level work directly into supervisory and control room operator positions. Sadly, and pathetically, these people were helping to diminish my operating sins by doing equally stupid things.

Jimmy McMaster, the control room operator I met on my first day at the plant, was one of these people. We were now on shift together. His operating ability was poor, but he was relatively smart and learned quickly. He was one of the people who had many years of experience doing a low-level job prior to coming to Four Corners. Because of his many years of experience, he was quickly moved into the control room... *A position he was not yet ready to do.* He was my control room operator after I went on shift. Again, it was a case of the blind leading the blind. He was as inexperienced as a control room operator as I was as an auxiliary operator.

Overtime was rampant and obligatory during this time at Four Corners. It wasn't a matter of when you worked overtime; it was a matter of when you **DIDN'T** work overtime. There was so much overtime on the plant site that they built a "free" restaurant with full-time fry cooks to feed the scads of people constantly working overtime. Rather than giving you a meal ticket like they did at Bridger, they would just fix you a steak and fries.

APS bought high-quality food and then allowed it to be violated by "chefs" who were barely minimum wage employees. How many ways can you ruin a large rib-eye Steak? They knew them all. I would often opt for frozen, store-bought burritos in lieu of some of the food they ruined by inflicting cookery on it. There was absolutely nothing they would not deep-fry… *Poorly.*

You might think I am exaggerating… However, dropping an expensive rib-eye steak into a deep-fat fryer and cooking it to oblivion is not being a chef. Everything was fried, and to ensure no one was subject to food poisoning, fried thoroughly. There was no medium or medium rare. It was cooked through until it was greasy shoe leather.

During the early part of my tenure on units 1, 2, and 3, I saw a fair amount of Harley Kelly. I would see him at work when I was on dayshift and occasionally see him and Loren at their house. His flaws became more glaring as we began to know him better. Loren appeared to be a good mother and a genuinely nice person, but Harley had some huge personal issues. He drank like a fish, never let honesty stop him from anything, and had a relatively pronounced drug habit. My tolerance for Harley ended somewhat abruptly.

It was a Friday, and I was working the PM shift (3:00 till 11:00). Harley was there working overtime and sought me out at about 7:30 PM that evening. He pulled me into the instrument shop and closed the door. It was obvious he had something on his mind.

"Are you the operator doing the river pumphouse run tomorrow or Sunday?" He seemed serious and did not exhibit his usual nervous laugh.

"I think I am doing it on Sunday. Why?" I was a bit concerned because his demeanor was so serious.

"I am working overtime tomorrow, and I need a favor from you. A **BIG** favor." He paused and looked intensely into my eyes with his head slightly tipped back.

"What is it you need?" I asked pensively. I knew something was up.

"I just need you to take the operator's truck to the pumphouse, but with one quick stop." He looked past me and down the hallway and then looked around before lowering his voice and continuing. "About a mile after you drop onto the APS road down into the river canyon, there is a large outcropping of boulders sitting next to the road. On the back side of these rocks is a hollowed-out opening in the sand between the two largest rocks. I will hide some instruments in the back of the Operator's truck, and I need you to put them in this hollowed-out area behind the rocks." He stared intensely at me to gauge my reaction.

"Wow. What would happen if we were caught doing this?" I knew it was a stupid question. I was shocked that he asked me to do this.

"Nobody is getting caught!" He quickly retorted. "I have this all planned. The instruments are small, and I can completely hide them in the back bed of the pick-up. It is full of shit all the time, and hiding my stuff won't be a problem. Besides, the idiot guards wouldn't know if this stuff is supposed to be in the back of the truck even if they bothered to look." Harley was right. The guards never checked the pickup for anything on the river run.

The Four Corners plant is built next to Morgan Lake. This large reservoir was built in the early 1960's to cool the plant condensers. The reservoir is filled from the San Juan River pump station that, by road, is about 6 miles away. The pump house is located at the foot of a small, narrow gorge and contains several massive pumps that move the water from the San Juan River to Morgan Lake.

The pump station required plant operators to check it regularly to ensure that the huge, vertical pumps and motors had adequate oil levels and were running normally. Sometimes it was necessary to stop and start the pumps locally. Because of the extreme weather that can be experienced in the high desert area of Four Corners, all the mechanical and electrical equipment is housed inside a large building at the foot of the gorge on the river.

Most of the operators liked the river pump station duty. It got you away from the plant for a couple of hours, and usually it was just a matter of making some equipment checks and then sitting in the metal circuit breaker enclosure and doing nothing. I didn't mind going there, but I was already dreading going there on Sunday. I had a pained look on my face as the thought of doing Harley's "favor" raced through my brain.

"Relax!" Harley said, interrupting my thoughts. "Nothing is going to happen. I have done this before, and it is a no-brainer. No one is getting caught."

"Okay," I said quietly. I was already mad at myself for not standing up to Harley. "I will do it."

"Great. I will touch base with you Sunday before you leave for the pumphouse." He looked a bit irritated as he continued. "Don't even give this any thought because no one is getting caught. This is not a big issue. *I do it all the time.*"

His assurances did little to comfort me. The rest of the day was wrecked as his request coursed continuously through my mind. What if he did this kind of thing so much that they were onto him, and this was the time they wised-up?" I would lose my job. Heck, I could go to jail over this. The more I thought about it, the more upset I became. I should have stood-up to Harley and just said no. I felt like the biggest wimp ever to live. I was making myself sick thinking about it. That night, I found it very easy to drink my anger away. Alcohol seemed to effectively take care of these situations.

Sunday afternoon came, and I was sincerely hoping that one of the units would trip or something would happen that would derail my trip to the pumphouse. There was no such luck. It was a quiet Sunday afternoon (for Four Corners), and my pumphouse run was imminent.

Harley found me out in the plant doing my equipment checks. He chose the air compressor building to rendezvous with me. The small units at Four Corners blew soot from the boiler tube surfaces with air and not steam. This required several very, very large and noisy air compressors located in a separate building nestled in the bowels of the plant.

"How are you doing?" Harley hollered over the metallic thumping of the huge reciprocating air compressors.

I hollered back, "good! Just checking equipment." I was intentionally not looking at him. I was still struggling with his request.

"You going to the pumphouse this evening?" He had an irritating smirk on his face. I wanted to smack him.

"Yeah. In about an hour." I looked away from him again. Deep down, I wanted to convey that I was pissed at him asking me to do this. Unfortunately, he never took the bait... If he did, he refused to show it.

He answered in a half-hearted mocking tone. "Sounds good. Enjoy the trip." He then turned and left the building.

I never looked in the back of the operator's pickup before leaving the plant. I just left the plant and headed for the pump station. I found the rock outcropping he described and quickly pulled over and parked the truck.

After carefully looking in every direction for headlights, I rummaged through the pick-up bed and found the instruments hidden there. There was a Simpson clamp-on voltmeter and a couple of other instruments I did not readily identify. I didn't take the time to study them. I quickly ran around the rocks using my flashlight and found the area he had dug out between the two largest rocks. I set the devices in the hole and immediately jumped back into the pickup, out of breath and fully sick to my stomach. I hated this. I vowed then that I was done with Harley. I was not going to jail with him or for him.

I drank myself to sleep after driving home that night. I made the decision that I would never do anything like this again. I didn't get so much as a thanks from Harley. I avoided him like the plague from that moment forward. I know that theft from these plants was a common thing. I had watched it at Bridger, and I knew it was going on at Four Corners, but this was my first time being involved, and I vowed it was my last time.

My drinking was becoming more problematic. I was to the point that a drink in the morning would ward off any hangover from the night before. I am certain Vangie did not know just how much I was drinking because she would have said something.

Shift work was getting the better of me. I had to drink to sleep and then take a drink to start the next day, depending on my shift. I continued to make stupid mistakes at the plant. The worst was tripping the induced draft fans on unit - 1, which shut the plant down.

I was on a graveyard shift, standing in the normally unmanned scrubber control room. Out of sheer boredom and trying to stay awake, I started fiddling with the vibration monitoring device for the induced draft fans. I am not exactly sure what I did, but alarms sounded, and immediately Jim McMaster's panicked voice pierced the plant paging system.

"UNIT – 1 BOILER IS POSITIVE!!! UNIT – 1 BOILER IS POSITIVE!!!" There was a momentary reprieve and then, *"MARK GREGG CALL THE CONTROL ROOM, MARK GREGG CALL THE CONTROL ROOM!!!"*

As soon as I heard the huge, induced draft fans trip, I ran from the scrubber control room because I knew if I got caught, it would be curtains for my job. I ran to a paging phone by the unit – 1 pulverizers.

"What's up, Jim? The mills just tripped!" I tried to sound like I normally would after a trip, but my heart was about to beat out of my chest.

"Unit – 1 I.D. fans tripped. *ARE YOU OKAY?*" He sounded panicked, but it struck me that he was more concerned about my well-being than the condition of the unit.

"Yeah, I am fine. I am down by the pulverizers."

He quickly exclaimed, "I was worried that you might be doing a slag check on the boiler and got burned by the positive furnace pressure." He seemed to be honestly concerned. *This made me feel even worse.*

"Any idea what caused the fans to trip?" I asked nervously, worried sick that someone might have seen me in the scrubber control room.

"I got an alarm that said high vibration on the 'A' I.D. fan, and then it tripped. This apparently overloaded the other one, which tripped, tripping the F.D. fans. We are offline. It was probably a slurry carryover from the scrubber into the fan. Alan called the instrument shop to check the level instruments in the scrubber."

A chill went down my spine, and I breathed a sigh of relief that he thought it was a slurry carryover. I couldn't believe what I just did. The cost to APS for this trip and the subsequent restart would probably pay my salary for years. I really screwed up again. This was way worse than the boiler sight glass blowout. I decided to act like everything was normal and pray no one saw me in the scrubber control room.

"I will open the boiler drains and get ready for a restart." I paused and took a deep breath before continuing. "Let me know if you find out what tripped the fans. I will go and check them for a restart."

We were unable to get the unit back on before leaving that morning. The next night, I heard that the *official* explanation of the trip was possible slurry carryover into the fan from the scrubber. Wow! Dodged a huge bullet on this one. I was so depressed. Graveyard shift depressed me, and then when I did stupid things, it depressed me even more. I hated graveyard shifts, and I hated doing stupid things even more. However, *I was so good at it.*

Life muddled on for a few more weeks. I made it back to afternoon shifts again. This was my favorite shift. I could drink myself to sleep and then get up late the next morning. Vangie and I were getting along okay, and I loved playing with Brandi, but overall, my life was crap. Things didn't seem right. I was solving everything with alcohol, and the control room operator's job seemed a million miles away.

It was my turn that Saturday afternoon to go to the river pumphouse again. I was relieved that I didn't have anything to deliver to the rock hiding place for Harley. I made a focused effort to stay as far away from him as I could. Even if he had asked, I knew for certain I would have refused to be a mule for him again.

The drive to the pumphouse was uneventful. However, as I ascended into the short gorge to the pump building, a chill went down my back. Something seemed wrong. I could not put my finger on it. Something just seemed wrong and foreboding. I pulled into the small parking area and shut the truck off. I could hear the high-pitched whine of the massive pumps inside the building. For no apparent reason, I became terrified. I wanted to start the truck and go back to the plant. I don't have a clue as to why, but I was panicking. I felt surrounded by pure, abject evil. A sense of total dread, almost death, was overwhelming me. I couldn't even force myself to get out of the truck for several more minutes. I was fully overcome with extreme terror and hopelessness. The feeling of horror was so overwhelming I became sick to my stomach.

I was fighting the urge to start the truck and speed out of the gorge and just say I checked things when I really didn't. Unfortunately, the operators were required to call the plant control room after arriving at the pump station and call again when they left. I was forced to go inside the pump house to make the mandatory phone call.

After making myself get out of the pickup, I hesitantly skulked over and slowly opened the metal door to the pumphouse with a flashlight in my hand as I kept looking around. I am not certain what I was looking for, but it felt like I was being swallowed by pure evil. I continued to be in a total, abject state of panic and had absolutely no idea why. I was struggling to fill my lungs with air. My fear was palpable and paralyzing.

My heart was beating out of my chest as I slipped quickly into the noisy pumphouse, immediately locking the door behind me. My skin was now crawling, and a deep, visceral, cold shiver went up my back. The feeling of horror bore down on me worse inside the pumphouse than in the truck. I could not grasp why I was bathed in sheer, unmitigated terror. Droplets of sweat were rolling down my cheeks as I stood there with my back against the steel door.

53

I was desperately trying to summon the courage to move further into the pumphouse. I was morbidly cold, and my hands were visibly shaking. I, verbally, *out loud*, tried to tell myself that what I was feeling made no sense whatsoever... That my feeling of sheer terror was unmerited.

Unable to shake the debilitating anxiety, I moved quickly past the large screaming pumps and into the messy, magazine-strewn circuit breaker cubicle where the operators sat before returning to the plant. I picked up the phone, called the plant control room, and told Jim McMaster I was there. I asked him if anything was going on at the plant, but he said that it was relatively quiet.

The feeling of a deep, acrid darkness surrounded me. I was certain it was going to swallow me into an inescapable living hell. It was so strong it was forcing my head down. Struggling to breathe, I knew I must go back into the pump area and check the pumps. I was engulfed in an utter terror that was enveloping me and squeezing the essence of life from my soul. I realized then I was dying. I was gasping for air that was not there. I was slowly suffocating and could not fight against it.

On the wooden table sitting in the circuit breaker cubicle was a small booklet amidst several magazines, including some porno magazines. It was a *"Chick Tract."* Chick Tracts were small, illustrated, evangelical booklets produced by a man named Jack Chick. One of the Navajo operators at the plant named, George Kelly (no relation to Harley) would leave these little cartoon books everywhere for people to read. I had read a few of them in the past.

This particular one was called *"THIS WAS YOUR LIFE"*. I picked it up and slowly read through the illustrated pages. It was about a man who died, and then his entire life was reviewed by God. He had not accepted Christ and was thrown into hell. Normally, I would have ignored the message because I had accepted Christ as my Lord and was even baptized when I was young. However, this was not a normal situation. The absolute soul-gripping *horror* I was experiencing was so real and so pervasive I could not stand it. As I finished reading the tract, I dropped to my knees on the steel floor of the circuit breaker cubicle and started praying loudly.

"Lord, Lord, I don't know what is happening to me right now. I don't know what is wrong. I think I am dying. I don't even know what I did. I NEED HELP RIGHT NOW. I DESPERATELY NEED HELP! PLEASE HELP ME! PLEASE DELIVER ME FROM THIS DARKNESS I AM FEELING. I WANT TO SEE VANGIE AND BRANDI AGAIN. PLEASE HELP ME!" Hot tears were streaming down my face, stinging my cheeks as I pleaded for help. *"Lord, show me a better way. I cannot continue the path I am on. I NEED YOUR HELP. PLEASE HELP ME!"*

I don't know how long I pleaded and prayed, but the overwhelming feeling of evil subsided. I felt like I could breathe again. I sat for a while in the switchgear room before calling the plant and telling them I was leaving. I was drained. I still felt the darkness, but it wasn't consuming me as it was when I arrived. I didn't have a clue what happened or what was happening. I slowly exited the pumphouse, locked the door, and proceeded back to the plant in a complete and utter daze.

The rest of the evening was surreal. I was so tired I could hardly do my equipment checks. I wasn't sleepy, I was tired. There is a huge difference. I couldn't have slept had I had the opportunity. I just didn't have any energy. Driving back to Farmington that night, I tried to figure out what happened. It made no sense. I even considered that I might be losing my mind.

The feeling of evil, dread, or horror was real. I did not make it up. Where did it come from? I don't know. I just know what I felt and how strongly I felt it. It made no sense. The only thing that made it subside was when I dropped to my knees and began praying. I ruminated on this all the way home.

Arriving at the house that night was different. I had no desire to have a drink. None. I don't know why. I just did not feel like having a drink. I was still exhausted from the events of the evening and decided to go straight to bed. Vangie commented on how tired I looked. I didn't say anything about the events of the evening to her. This was out of character for me. I normally told Vangie **EVERYTHING**. I just told her I didn't feel well and went to bed.

I awakened the next morning and was extremely thirsty. Not just a little thirsty. I felt deathly parched or dehydrated. I tried to drink some water, but it tasted terrible. I felt like apple juice. In fact, I was absolutely *craving* apple juice. We had a Piggly Wiggly a couple of blocks away from 1037 Zuni Street. I drove there and bought a gallon of Skyline© (brand) Apple Juice. It was from the Delta, Colorado, area, so I thought I would try it.

The apple juice tasted amazing to me. I was craving it so badly that I drank almost half of the gallon jug. I went to work that afternoon, still craving apple juice. I got off work and came home that night and drank the remaining half gallon. The next morning, I went to Piggly Wiggly and got another gallon. This time, I drank most the gallon before the end of the day. This craving was insatiable. Initially, it did not even register to me that I was not drinking alcohol. As expensive as the apple juice was, it was cheaper than the alcohol that I had been buying.

The craving for apple juice continued for several months. I was drinking a gallon or more a day. Some days, I would drink close to two gallons. When we moved from Farmington, the single-car garage at 1037 Zuni Street was filled with gallon apple juice jugs! Oddly, during this same time, I lost all desire to drink alcohol. In fact, I completely stopped drinking alcohol. I didn't miss it. I didn't need it. I just craved and drank apple juice. I drank it because I continuously craved it. There was no rhyme or reason for this. It was just a simple fact for me. For several months, I drank virtually nothing else, including water.

About a month before moving from Farmington, I awakened one morning, and the thought of drinking apple juice almost gagged me. As fast as the craving came upon me, it left me in the same manner. Since that day I have not had any desire ever to drink apple juice again. It did something for me, though. Somehow, it killed all desire for alcoholic beverages. I stopped drinking beer, wine, and hard alcohol. More than this, I never missed it after that.

Many years later, I read that sometimes alcoholism is related to a sugar imbalance in a person's body. Maybe this is what happened. I do know that apple juice is sugar laden. I still find it fascinating that in one day, I lost all my alcohol cravings, and in one day, I lost all my apple juice cravings. I cannot provide any explanation other than the truth of what happened. I didn't know it then, but it would start making sense later.

~5~
Finally, Control Room Operator

A few weeks after my experience at the river pump house, APS posted a control room operator job opening. It wasn't for units 1, 2, and 3. It was for units 4 and 5. These things were beasts. They were B&W super-critical boilers and General Electric cross-compound turbine/generators. They operated with a turbine throttle steam pressure of 3600 psig. To put things in perspective, either unit – 4 or unit – 5 at Four Corners would generate over 1 million horsepower when operating at full load. They were over 4.5 times larger than each of the small units at Four Corners.

I applied for the control room operator position on units 4, and 5, knowing I had almost no chance of getting the position because I had zero experience on the bigger units. Heck, I had only a few months' experience on the smaller units and an *appalling* reputation to boot. I just applied for the position to let management know I was interested. *At the time, the irony was lost on me.* Plus, it gave me a chance to take the unit 4 and 5 control room operator exam to see how complex it was.

The test was another no-brainer test. Even though I knew nothing (or very little) about the super-critical units, the test seemed ridiculously easy to me. In fact, I thought it was a joke. However, it was no joke. There were only two other people bidding on the job, and neither of them passed the test. This left management with only one choice. *ME!*

If it had not been a union plant, they would have indeed bypassed me and went outside and hired someone with experience. However, because it was a union plant, they had to go by the union contract. The contract simply stated that job positions would be filled from the inside, and they were obligated to fill with the senior person who passed the position testing.

While I was not a union-minded person (frankly, I hated unions), I appreciated that it was there as it forced them to give me the control room operator position. It is important to understand just how ridiculous it was to award this position to me. I had no knowledge or experience with these huge, highly complex plants, and yet they were forced by the union to hire me.

I was moved almost immediately to units 4 and 5 on the "C" crew. Bob Everett was the sage, experienced Shift Supervisor. He had been with APS since Moby Dick was a minnow. He started in the Ocotillo Plant in Phoenix and then came to Four Corners for the start-up of units 4, and 5. I liked him. He was low-key, seemed to be a good leader, and his plant experience was excellent.

There were two Shift Foreman. One was Richard Kiering. He was young, brash and a lanky 6 ½ foot tall bean pole. When I say young, he was probably 30 or 35 years old. This was *very* young for a supervisor in a plant like this. He was not well-liked because he was quite full of himself. There was nothing he didn't know about this plant. All you had to do was ask him, and he would tell you so. Then there was Dicky. Dicky Mundt was a conundrum to me. He took a personal interest in supervising me.

Dicky was in his late 40s and looked much like an overstuffed scarecrow with a wrinkled jack-o-lantern head. His hair was short and intensely curly. Maybe he permed it. I just don't know. He wore thick, black-framed glasses. His left eye was higher than his right eye, probably not enough to be considered a birth defect, but enough to be noticeable. His teeth were a disaster. They were strewn about in his mouth in no particular fashion or order, and most of them were random sizes. When he smiled, he looked surprisingly like a flesh-colored jack-o-lantern.

Dicky had extensive knowledge and experience on units 4, and 5, although I'm not sure how intelligent he was. His most impressive attribute was his ability to speak English like a Navajo. He was continuously mocking the Navajos by speaking as one while saying really stupid, albeit hilarious, things. He did not hide this questionable trait from the Navajo's. In fact, he would intentionally use it right to their faces to belittle them on a regular basis. He was a world-class ass.

Dicky was also the father to Ronny Mundt. Ronny was one of the two other operators that bid the control room operator position but failed the test and was not considered for the job. Essentially, I took the control room operator position away from his son, who had spent several years as an Auxiliary Operator on units 4, and 5. I think Dicky wouldn't have minded this as much as he did if I had deserved the position.

Unfortunately, in my first week on units – 4, and 5, Dicky ushered me around the plant and "trained me" while asking me tons and tons of questions about my life and the operation of power plants.

Each subsequent day of that first week, his opinion of me appeared to diminish. By the end of the first week, I was nothing more than a *white Navajo* to him. He obviously heard about my many mistakes at units 1, 2, and 3. After spending a fair amount of time with me during the first week, he deemed me far inferior to his son. I can assure you he was correct. I could not compete with someone who had spent substantial time on these large, complex units.

Dicky's dislike of me was deep and he was willing to go to great lengths to punish me for taking his son's control room job away from him. I had quite a ride with Dicky as my Shift Foreman. Fortunately, I was so wrapped-up in trying to learn as much as could about units 4 and 5 that I didn't fixate on my woes with Dicky.

I was overwhelmed with the size and complexity of the equipment on units 4, and 5, but did as much as I possibly could to learn these units. I worked in the Auxiliary Operator position for about 6 weeks before moving into the control room. This was barely enough time to even know where all the equipment was located. However, I absolutely loved the control room for units 4, and 5. They also used miniature controls, but the sheer amount of equipment and complexity made the control boards much larger than units 1, 2, and 3. The annunciator (alarm) panels were large like Bridger's, but everything else was very small. It was a noisy control room. As with unit 1, 2, and 3's control room, it sat on the mezzanine deck and not the operating deck. The control room was literally buried in the bowels of the plant.

My first official day in the control room was a night shift. I finished my time as an Auxiliary Operator on our final day shift and then started in the control room on our first graveyard shift. I wasn't worried about being sleepy because I was always wide awake on the first night shift, it was the subsequent night shifts that I miserably slid into hell. Plus, I was so excited about being in the control room that I could hardly contain myself. *This was it.* I finally had the control room operator's position I had dreamed about for years!

As an Auxiliary Operator I would go to work in grubby clothes because you were never able to return from the plant clean. Between coal dust, ash, oil, grease, and general grime, you were usually dirty as an Auxiliary Operator. However, as a Control Room Operator, you could go to work clean and come home clean.

My first day as a control room operator, I proved to be a completely ignorant, 22-year-old kid. I wore a pair of baggy, straight-legged, light green, obnoxious plaid pants with 1" leg cuffs. I complemented the slacks with a pastel yellow button-up shirt and my favorite "dress" shoes. They were screaming yellow tennis shoes with black stripes on the side. They looked suspiciously like large bumblebees on my feet. I was a scrawny, blonde kid that looked about 16 or 17 years old. The average age for a control room operator was probably 30 to 40 years old.

Dicky started the night with a vengeance. I honestly think my apparel added to his rage of taking Ronny's job. After shift turn-over was complete, he approached me with a goofy, disheveled grin on his jack-o-lantern head.

"You're in the big league now, kid." He came up behind me and cupped my head on both sides with his wrinkled, puffy hands and forcibly twisted it toward the unit – 4 control board. "See this?" Before I could answer, he continued. "I'm gonna give you a learning enema. I want you to memorize every single switch, button, light, and the location of every single controller on this board."

"That's my plan!" I tried to not act surprised at his actions. Unfortunately, he wasn't finished yet.

"You're too damn ignorant to have a plan! Besides, it don't matter how well you learn where everything is in this control room. You *STILL* won't have a single clue how to operate this plant. Learning how to operate this plant will take you years and years, and I hope we all live through it."

He then laughed a sinister, insincere laugh, turned, and walked towards the Shift Foreman's office. About half-way there, he looked back and said, "At 0400 I want you to have every major component on the board memorized. I am going to test you on it. In the meantime, no matter what happens, don't you dare touch one damn thing. If you have an issue, let Larry handle it." He then went into the Shift Foreman's office and closed the door.

Larry Clarke gave me a weak, reassuring smile and said, "he's not that bad a guy, better just do what he says."

I felt like I was handcuffed. It didn't matter what alarm sounded or what happened, Larry slid over from unit − 5's controls and handled unit − 4. It wouldn't have been all that bad if he would have told me what he was doing. He would just do it and go back to unit − 5. Apparently, I was the bastard child and was resigned to being a place-taker and not a real operator. In hindsight, I didn't know anything about this plant, and they were fully justified in treating me this way.

Dicky, Rich Kiering, and Bob Everett were in and out of the control room continuously because there was always something requiring attention to keep these massive iron behemoths operating. I was virtually invisible. They talked over me, around me, and behind me but never *to me*. At least when I was doing the Auxiliary Operator job, we communicated occasionally.

At about 5:00 that morning, Dicky came back into the control room. He had a large rag that looked like an old hand towel. He came over to me and told me to turn around. Upon turning my back to him, he threw the partially rolled-up towel over my head and pulled it tight, completely blindfolding me. I was surprised, shocked, and tried to resist, but Dicky was a large, powerful man. He tied a knot so tightly that the towel was blocking even the slightest light out and was actually painful.

"Okay, here's the plan." He grabbed my shoulders and aggressively muscled me over to what seemed to be the left side of unit – 4's control board. "I have you in front of the pulverizer controls. I am going to call out different buttons and controllers for the pulverizers and you will **IMMEDIATELY** place your fingers within an inch or two of it or you will receive the booby prize…" His voice trailed off, and he gave me a menacing laugh.

Each unit had 8 pulverizers. The controls consisted of numerous pushbuttons for each mill that had to be activated in the correct sequence to properly start it There were also three Bailey 721 controllers for each mill that required operator manipulation in the correct order while pushing the appropriate buttons to start the unit. Each controller adjusted and controlled the primary air flow, the primary air temperature, and the coal feeder speed on each pulverizer.

Therefore, there were 24 controllers bunched together on the "bench" section of the board, plus the pushbuttons for each pulverizer that were located above the controllers on the vertical section of the board. This was JUST the pulverizers. There was another section of the board for the forced draft and primary air fans, a section for the condensate system, a section for the feedwater system, a section for the steam control and bypass system, a section for the turbine, and a section for the generator. This amounted to a huge number of controllers, buttons and switches crammed together in a very small space. Good thing I had eyesight and could SEE each controller and switch. Oh, right... *I was blindfolded by a mean, vengeful lunatic.*

Dicky pushed me hard against the bench board section and barked, "D pulverizer burner gates pushbutton!" I was picturing in my mind where the D pulverizer block of buttons was on the vertical section of the board when Dicky's huge right hand grabbed me below the rib cage and above the waist and pinched the living hell out of me. It hurt so bad my eyes teared-up. I jerked away.

Before I could say anything, Dicky immediately barked, "F pulverizer motor start button!" I was disorientated, disheveled, and pissed. Almost immediately, he grabbed and pinched me again, less hard, but it still hurt like crazy. I ripped the blindfold off and turned towards Dicky.

Before I could say anything, he blurted out, "*Not ready, are you? What the hell have you been doing the last 4 hours?*" His eyes looked demonic. He spun around and headed for the Shift Foreman's office, looking over his shoulder at me. "Next time I tell you to be ready, you damn sure better be ready!"

I stood stunned, hurting, embarrassed, and pissed. My dignity had been ripped from me, leaving me in a pile of my own misery. Larry Clark looked at me and bluntly said, "Probably ought to memorize the board a little better."

I stared at the board in a daze until shift turnover. I was again ignored during the shift turnover as the incoming operator for unit – 4 talked directly to Larry Clarke while I just stood there brooding. I went home that morning depressed and angry. This was NOT how this was supposed to be.

The subsequent month was grueling, painful, and frustrating. Dicky's antics and dislike for me intensified. Dicky's physical abuse continued unabated. I was bruised up and down my sides and on my arms. My dislike for Dicky was multiplying daily. While I was rapidly learning about the plant, his methods were barbaric and inexcusable. Vangie was getting concerned with all the bruises on my arms and rib area.

Larry Clarke was getting tired of running both units, so he began spending some time teaching me. I learned to start and stop the pulverizers and tips on doing load changes. Dicky even started giving me some decent pointers on how some of the unit controls worked. However, the humiliation continued every chance Dicky could arrange it. One of the most embarrassing episodes was largely self-inflicted after I was "set up" for it by Dicky and Richard Kiering.

Rich Kiering came nonchalantly into the control room on an afternoon shift and asked me to go to the cafeteria trailer and get him a burrito. That, in itself, was demeaning. I was not an Auxiliary Operator any longer. I was a Control Room Operator. We weren't supposed to leave the control room. I wasn't supposed to be his gopher. Unfortunately, I didn't have a clue it was all a set-up. I begrudgingly grabbed my hard hat and left the control room for the cafeteria trailer.

When I returned with his burrito, He, Dicky, Larry, and a couple of the Auxiliary Operators were sitting around the control room and passing a sophisticated-looking device that appeared to be a precision brass instrument of some sort. On the top was a small paddle wheel that, when a person wrapped their lips around the feed tube and blew into it, the paddle wheel would turn very slowly. The body of this purported "lung-tester" was a brass drum that you held with your hand, much like you would a smoker's pipe. You would then blow into it as hard as possible while counting the revolutions of the paddle wheel in a thirty-second period.

Without saying a word to me, they were passing the "lung-tester" around the control room. Each person would wipe the feed tube with a towel and then puff their cheeks and turn beet red as they blew into the device with as much force as they could muster. They would laugh and carry on and then try it again and again to see if they could beat their previous attempts. No one asked me to do it. They just passed it between them and timed each blow as they counted the revolutions. As I watched, I became increasingly curious about how well I would do. After all, I was younger than any of them and I didn't smoke like most of them.

When I could no longer contain my curiosity, I said, "Give me a shot at this. I will put you old farts to shame." They all laughed and then handed me the device and the rag to wipe the mouthpiece. After cleaning it as best I could, I held it to my face, wrapped my lips around the feed tube, drew an inordinate amount of air into my young, powerful lungs and blew as if my life depended upon it. I was going to show these jerks that I could do *something* well.

Instantly, I was blinded by a thick, biting, black cloud surrounding my head and covering my face, filling my eyes and nose with a stinging, oily black powder. I was violently coughing, and my eyes stung like they were on fire. I couldn't see a thing. I could hear them all laughing hysterically. Dicky finally grabbed me by the arm and yanked me into the restroom, helping me clean-up as best I could, all the while laughing his guts out.

It seems there was a small hole in the center of the feed tube that you covered with the tip of your tongue as you blew into the periphery. If you plugged the hole, the air was pushed through a channel on the periphery to the paddle wheel that would slowly spin from the escaping air. If you did not plug the center hole, the air blew freely and rapidly into the brass body and blew whatever was loaded into the hopper **STRAIGHT BACK INTO YOUR FACE!** In my case, it was *lamp black*, a finely ground petroleum-based carbon powder.

The dense, heavy powder ruined my shirt, and it was impossible to completely clean off my face. I looked as if I had thick mascara around my eyes for a couple of days. *I was so proud...* Seriously, the humiliation was almost unbearable. Much like the sight glass blowout on unit – 2, I was now the butt of all jokes on units 4, and 5. Once again, random people on the plant site would see me and flash a thumbs-up as they grinned maliciously.

Fortunately for me, units 4 and 5 were not running well for several months. They were having extreme issues with boiler fouling that continuously shut down the plant requiring intensive boiler clean-ups. The units were also suffering from serious foundation settling issues that required mud-jacking to keep the equipment and steelwork in plumb. Apparently, Morgan Lake saturated the layers of earth around the gargantuan plant and caused the foundation to abnormally settle.

Due to the mud-jacking, large feedwater and steam pipes carrying high temperature and pressure water and steam would quickly go out of alignment, bend pipe hangers and put valves and piping in precarious positions. Because of this, we were constantly tripping and/or shutting down and then restarting the units after they made temporary fixes.

I was receiving substantial, albeit random, experience coming on shift in the middle of start-ups and shutdowns. Even if they did not let me do any operating, I was closely watching all the operational iterations on the unit and learning a lot more about the plant. My turn to be "in the barrel" (Dicky's words) was coming upon me like a speeding freight train, and I was too ignorant to realize how big and powerful that train really was!

~6~

Disaster Upon Disaster

The next set of day shifts proved to be challenging at best. I came in my first morning on the day shift and unit – 4 had just been released for cold clean-up.

Cold clean-up is a significant step on a super-critical unit because the water in the boiler and boiler circuits must be extremely clean. Water is called the "universal solvent" because it picks up a bit of anything it touches. Because of this, making it ultra-pure was a challenge.

Super-critical units use in-line condensate polishers. These are very large, pressure tanks filled with millions of tiny resin beads that deionize the water. The water that passes through the deionizers is so pure it will not conduct electricity. Virtually every single contaminant is removed in the deionizers. This is far beyond filtration. Deionizers work on the molecular level to clean the water. Everything involved with the condensate polishers is big, expensive, messy, and critical to the plant operation.

Cold clean-up involves bringing the condensate system online by using two of the three 1,250-horsepower condensate pumps to circulate water from the hotwell, through the low-pressure feedwater heaters, and up to the massive deaerator, which towers about 150 feet above the ground floor. That morning, the atmosphere in the plant was tense. Repeated shutdowns and start-ups had worn everyone thin, forcing long hours at the facility. Management was on edge as the persistent issues were costing APS a fortune. Dayshifts were especially tough, with all the managers present, alongside the full mechanical maintenance, electrical maintenance, and instrumentation teams, all working on equipment and constantly needing operations to step in. On a normal week, it felt chaotic—this week, it was complete pandemonium.

Immediately after completing shift turnover Dicky came over and looked at me with malice in his eyes.

"Can you handle putting unit – 4 in cold clean-up on your own or do I have to call someone in on overtime to babysit you?" His condescending attitude angered me, but I couldn't afford to show it. He then continued without me answering. "Larry is going to be completely tied up on unit – 5 doing turbine testing. We need to start the water clean-up on unit – 4. It is your unit. Can you handle it?"

"I think so." I paused to justify my existence. "There isn't that much to do in the control room. During shift turnover, the graveyard operator told me that they had everything aligned in the field." I tried to show him how confident I was because I was aching to do something on my own.

"Don't trust those bastards on "A" shift!" he growled with venom. I had been around Dicky long enough to know that every other shift was inferior to his. "You send your outside operator to walk down the entire condensate system and make sure it is lined up properly before you even consider starting your first condensate pump."

As he finished, Bob Everett stuck his head out of the Shift Supervisor's office door and told him he wanted to talk to him. Dicky put his finger in my face and said, "Don't *$#@ this up." He then went into Bob's office.

Woo Hoo! For the very first time, I was left on my own to do some actual operating. I was both excited and nervous. Harrison Begay was my Auxiliary Operator on unit – 4 that day. He was a Navajo operator who was pretty darn sharp and a hard worker. Dicky never treated him with any respect, but he was a good operator. I paged him and told him to check the entire condensate system for cold clean-up and to call me when the first condensate pump was throttled and ready to start.

The plant paging system was abuzz with activity. Between the start-up taking place on unit – 4, the turbine testing on unit – 5, plus the normal dayshift maintenance activities, the plant was noisy, and people were going in every direction, much like ants on an ant hill.

It took Harrison over an hour to recheck the condensate system to ensure it was ready for operation. All the low-pressure feedwater heaters had to be checked, including dozens of large manual valves, as well as the control valves for filling and maintaining the deaerator level. His final check was the three condensate pumps. At 1,250 horsepower each, these huge, vertical pumps moved a massive amount of water. Since the condensate system was drained, it was imperative to start the first condensate pump with a throttled discharge valve.

If you started one of these huge pumps without throttling the discharge valve, the resulting flow through the empty pipes and equipment would cause a massive, destructive water hammer. The lines and vessels absolutely must be filled slowly in a controlled fashion to prevent tearing lines off their hangers and damaging piping and vessels.

I was nervous enough about starting the first condensate pump that I studied the block of buttons where they were operated from. There were three start-buttons and three stop-buttons. They were backlighted, which means they changed colors to indicate the pump state (running or off).

The standard procedure was to throttle the "C" pump and start it first. This would slowly fill and pressurize the condensate system. Once the system was filled and pressurized, either of the other two pumps could be started with a wide-open discharge valve, and the throttled pump could be shut down. What could be easier?

I verified with Harrison that the "C" pump was throttled and ready to start. I took a deep breath and called out on the plant paging system, *"4C CONDENSATE PUMP COMING ON!"* I carefully pressed the START button for the 4C condensate pump. The lights in the control room instantly dimmed, and the control room physically convulsed with a cloud of dust falling from the drop-ceiling panels. There were several thunderous, shuddering booms in the plant as the control room floor shuddered. The plant paging system immediately went crazy.

"TRIP UNIT - 4 CONDENSATE PUMPS!!! TRIP UNIT - 4 CONDENSATE PUMPS!!!"

I had instant heart-lock as I mashed my finger on the stop button for the 4C condensate pump. I immediately noticed there was a red light on both 4A and 4B condensate pumps, indicating they were also running, which made no sense to me. I then mashed the stop buttons on them. The plant went silent for a moment. Larry Clarke ran over from the unit – 5 control board.

"What the hell did you do!!!" He screamed at me, looking perplexed and angry. Before I could answer, Bob Everett ran out of the Shift Supervisor's office to the unit – 4 control board as a call rang out over the plant paging system that chilled my blood to the bone.

"MEDICAL ASSISTANCE REQUIRED AT UNIT – 4 CONDENSATE POLISHERS! MEDICAL ASSISTANCE REQUIRED AT UNIT – 4 CONDENSATE POLISHERS!"

I was numb and in shock. Everything happened so fast, and I had no clue what occurred. Bob Everett looked at me angrily and said, "What did you do?" He paused as he walked in front of me to the condensate section of the control board and barked, "Show me what you did, *RIGHT NOW!*"

I reached my finger towards the 4C condensate pump start button and said, "I just announced it and pressed the start button for the 4C condensate pump."

"WAS IT THROTTLED?" This was the first time I had ever seen him raise his voice.

"Yes, it was throttled, according to Harrison." I turned defensive for obvious reasons.

"DID YOU HOLD IN THE STOP BUTTONS FOR THE OTHER TWO PUMPS AS YOU STARTED THE THROTTLED PUMP?" His intense glare was boring right through me.

"NO. WHY WOULD I DO THAT?" I was totally dumbfounded by the revelation that I was apparently supposed to push the stop buttons on the other two pumps at the same time. Bob looked at Larry with both disgust and surrender in his eyes.

"Didn't *ANYONE* tell you about the low-pressure start on the out-of-service pumps?"

"No. I don't know what you are talking about." Bob lowered his head and shook it slowly. He then spoke to me in his more familiar, fatherly fashion.

"Mark, when any condensate pump is running, there is an automatic start function for the non-running pumps. If the condensate system pressure goes low, it automatically sends a start to the standby pumps to maintain condensate pressure." He pointed to the condensate pressure gage located above the pump start switches. "As soon as you started the throttled pump, the relays see only one pump in service with low condensate system pressure. Since the other two pumps are not running it immediately sends a start signal to the out-of-service pumps." He paused and then raised his voice. ***"YOU WERE SUPPOSED TO HOLD THE STOP BUTTONS IN ON 4A AND 4B PUMPS UNTIL THE CONDENSATE PRESSURE NORMALIZED."***

I was dumbstruck and stunned. No one had EVER said a word to me about this and I had never read anything about it. Before I could respond to Bob, someone called for him on the plant paging system. He picked up my handset and answered the call. I could not hear what was being said, but after a few minutes of back-and-forth discussion, I heard Bob ask the caller, "He is going to be okay, right?" Again, this chilled me to the bone.

Bob finished his call, turned towards me and stated sternly, "When all three condensate pumps started at the same time, the water hammer tore the condensate line from its hangars and blew out some flanges, but the biggest damage was to the polishers." He paused and shook his head. "It blew out the sight glasses and flanges on the polishers, flooding the basement with over a million dollars' worth of resin beads. The resin beads acted like tiny ball bearings, making the partially flooded basement floor slicker than snot." He took a deep breath. "Dicky was down by the pulverizers and went running into the polisher area to see what happened and slipped on the resin beads and apparently broke his arm."

I wanted to crack up laughing but knew this would be a serious mistake. I couldn't help but think that Dicky breaking his arm was a comeuppance for his treatment of me the past several weeks! As it turned out, Dicky just dislocated his arm from the shoulder joint. Nothing was broken, but he apparently had a painful ride into the Farmington hospital, where they put the arm back into the socket.

As for me, I never even got a disciplinary letter in my file. Why? How could I be punished for not doing something that no one ever mentioned had to be done? Let's see now, who was supposed to be training me? Right... *Dicky Mundt*. Woo Hoo! Not only did he have his arm dislocated, but Dicky also had to answer for letting me do such a stupid thing. It goes without saying that our relationship deteriorated even further after this incident.

My next major control room error was only a week or so later when I allowed the unit to trip due to a polisher unit exhausting. Unit – 4 was at full load. I was the unit – 4 control room operator, with Larry Clarke running unit – 5. An alarm sounded on the Unit – 4 chemistry board. I walked about 8 steps from the BTG (Boiler-Turbine-Generator) board to the chemistry board. The alarm was sounding because the condensate system pH was decreasing.

I sat and stared at the trend recorder for several minutes, trying to think of why the pH would be falling. While I was thinking about it, the unit tripped on high conductivity. The problem was simple, preventable, and commonplace. The in-service polishing unit had reached its "exhausted" state and was allowing cations to bleed into the condensate, quickly reducing the pH. All I needed to do was put the standby polisher unit into service. Nothing more. I did not do it, and the unit tripped.

Once again, I screwed up royally. Even though there was not a letter in my file because it was considered an internal training error, my dignity and any pride I might have was now, non-existent.

Every day at my "dream" job as a Control Room Operator plunged me further into the abyss of self-doubt. Unfortunately, due to my immaturity, I would overcompensate for my massive shortcomings by acting like I knew something. What's worse than being incompetent? Acting like you aren't to the very people who know you are. I had yet to learn about true humility and knowing when to admit you were wrong and then focus on doing better. I had figured out how to blame everyone else except me for my shortcomings. ***Essentially, I was becoming a politician***.

As an avid reader of *Power Magazine*, I always stayed informed about job opportunities in the utility industry. *Power Magazine* was a leading monthly publication for the electric utility sector, and in the pre-internet era, it served as the go-to source for job listings and industry updates.

Not long after committing several of my bone-headed mistakes, I noticed there was a job posting for new Control Room Operators at a large, three-unit plant under construction in eastern Wyoming. It was called the Laramie River Station. I was super excited because this brand-new plant was not running yet. The control room operators would be there many months prior to the plant becoming operational. I always remembered Joe Johnson saying that a single new unit start-up was the equivalent of 10 years of experience. This plant was going to be three brand new units. I could not mail my resume' to them any quicker than I did.

The company was Basin Electric Power Cooperative. It was headquartered in Bismarck, North Dakota. The plant was being constructed in Wheatland, Wyoming. Wheatland was a small farm community of about 2,000 people that was an hour or so north of Cheyenne, the Capital of Wyoming.

I figured it could never be as bad as Rock Springs. Unfortunately, I completely underestimated the impact of bringing approximately 10,000 construction workers (at the peak of construction) into a town of 2,000 people. It didn't matter. I was ready to kill if necessary to get a chance to do a new plant start-up. I knew I would never outrun my reputation here at Four Corners. I would have to leave the environment entirely. A new plant was exactly what I needed to redeem myself.

I did not see myself as anything more than a total screw-up at Four Corners. It was obvious that no one else did, either. A winding road of consistent, costly errors solidified my reputation. However, I think I was improving some. As time went by and we did more start-ups, I was learning the job and performing in almost a mediocre fashion… Except for the massive screw-ups that I seemed to step into repeatedly.

I certainly wasn't the only one with issues at the Four Corners Plant. The rate of alcoholism was extremely high on the reservation as well as among the Navajos working at the plant. Many lived on the reservation and didn't have telephones, so they couldn't call in "sick" when they weren't coming to work.

The quickest, most effective way to get fired at Four Corners was NOT calling in if you had to miss your shift for any reason. Usually, you receive one warning, and after that, you are fired if you don't show-up to work without the obligatory call-in. This left many of the Navajos at a disadvantage. The location of the closest phone to the plant for many of them was... *THE PLANT.*

Since units 4 and 5 were the closest to the employee parking lot, it was not unusual to have a drunken Navajo weave their way on the road(s) into the plant and park somewhere in the parking lot without hitting or damaging another car. After arriving, they would stagger from the parking lot to the Unit 4 & 5 water chemistry lab (laboratory) to call in sick for their shift. The laboratory was on the mezzanine deck (2nd floor) *RIGHT NEXT TO THE CONTROL ROOM*. The wall between the water lab and the control room was replete with windows.

We would routinely watch inebriated Navajos enter the laboratory, pick up the phone and dial the Shift Supervisor's office, which is on the other side of the control room, also replete with windows. When the Shift Supervisor would pick up the phone, they could look across the control room into the lab and *SEE* the person calling in "sick". Once they reported "sick", they would stagger/stumble back to the parking lot, get into their car, and leave... *What a system.*

Because APS did little at that time to train the Navajo workers, they had more than their share of problems and mistakes at the plant. Unfortunately, there was a double standard. The Navajos were almost expected to make mistakes, people like me were not. Therefore, I viewed my huge backlog of mistakes as effectively reducing the number of double standards. Funny thing... *I never received any thanks from the Navajo for my efforts.*

One typical evening shift, Larry and I were in the control room together. He was running unit – 5, and I was on a shut down on unit – 4. It seemed I always was on unit – 4 when things happened. There was no reason for this, it just seemed to be the luck of the draw.

While sitting in the control room reading a technical manual, there was a series of odd alarms and then the coal delivery system to the coal bunkers that ultimately feed the pulverizers, abruptly shut down. There were some random fire alarms and other miscellaneous system alarms. I didn't have a clue what caused all these alarms to come in at once.

Larry looked at me and said, "I think all of 4 and 5's coal system is powered by the general service electrical bus on units 1, 2, and 3. I wonder if they tripped some breakers over there."

"I don't have a clue," I answered quickly. "If you want, I can go over there and see what is happening." I figured, why not? My unit was down, and I was tired of reading.

Larry tried calling the 1, 2, and 3 control rooms, but oddly, no one answered. He then glanced over to the Shift Foreman's office to see if Rich Kiering or Dicky was there. The office was empty, and Bob Everett's office was also vacated. He looked back at me. "You just as well walk over and see what is happening. If someone needs something on unit – 4, I will handle it."

I grabbed my hard hat and bounded down the stairs. I was young and still in great shape so the stairs were my preferred transit to the lower floors of the plant. As soon as I got out of the pump room onto the main plant roadway, I could clearly hear safety valves lifting on the small units. Worse than this, I noticed the general service breaker cubicle was ***ON FIRE*** and sending billowing black smoke swirling high into the air.

Seeing the smoke and hearing the boiler safeties prompted me to speed up to a dead-run over the circulating water intake structure and through the door into unit – 3's pump room. It was dark, and water hammers were rattling the building. Insulation dust fell like a heavy snowstorm in the darkened pump room. Most of this insulation was asbestos. I don't know how much asbestos I have inhaled over the years, but it is probably a lot.

I quickly exited the pump bay and ran farther down towards unit – 2 where the control room for all three of the small units was located. Taking an external set of stairs, I sprinted to the mezzanine and into the practically dark control room. The only visible lighting was the emergency DC exit lights and a few emergency lights. The alarm panels for all three of the small units were ablaze with alarms, and all the alarm bells on each unit, including mystery alarms I had never heard before, were producing a nerve-rattling, in-your-face cacophony.

In the middle of the 1, 2, and 3 control-room horseshoe was Teddy Smallgorge. His name was appropriate. He was barely five feet tall and quite stocky, a gentle way of saying he was portly. He wore thick, round glasses and appeared completely stunned. It was obvious his units lost all incoming and outgoing power when the generators tripped, leaving them in a condition known as "black-plant". A black plant means there is no station service. The plant is dark or black, and you have little control over most of the system and processes. Black plants happen, and they are always unnerving and even dangerous.

Units 1, 2, and 3 were on a 230,000-volt switchyard distribution system. Units 4 and 5 were on a completely different 500,000-volt switchyard distribution system. Other than the coal supply system, units 4 and 5 were largely unaffected by the power loss on the small units.

I looked directly at Teddy. He was just standing there, slowly blinking his eyes in a dazed, semi-synchronous fashion. It was surreal. I raised my voice over the din of the alarms and the background of the safety valves. *"TEDDY, YOUR GENERAL SERVICE BUS IS ON FIRE DOWN THERE!"*

Teddy gave me a completely disheveled look and said, *"OH... DEY-CAWED-AN-SED-LITTO-BILDING-ON-FIRE."* At that moment, he seemed to be struggling with English. *"DERE-LOTS-ALARMS-NOT SHUR-WUT-DO."*

I tried acknowledging some of the dozens of alarms, but it was fruitless. Until power was restored, the plant was in bad shape. I knew I was considered the enemy after moving to units 4, and 5, and my sketchy reputation in the small units certainly didn't help matters.

I felt bad for Teddy because he was dazed and confused while everyone was out assessing the damage. However, I left him there alone anyway. I figured everyone was trying to figure out how to restore power to the units, and there was nothing I could do until power was returned to the plant. I left the control room and went back to 4 and 5 and told Larry everything that was happening.

Later, it was determined that a feral cat had found its way into the electrical bus work through a missing inspection door. The poor cat had a shocking experience, and the plant suffered a multi-million-dollar, triple-unit shutdown because some lazy electrician didn't take the time to bolt an inspection door back into place. A few scraps of burned fur were the only evidence of the perpetrator. I doubt he suffered for more than a millisecond or so.

The failure of APS to properly train Navajos was steeped in the prevailing attitude that Navajos were impossible to train. This, of course, is total rubbish. Once APS committed to proper training for the Navajos, they became productive, effective employees.

Not unlike the whites or any other ethnic group, some were easier to train than others. The only major obstacle that seemed to plague many of the Navajos was alcoholism. Apart from this, they were as capable of operating and maintaining a powerplant as anyone else when trained to do so.

The next big disaster and it was a dilly, further engulfed me in my seemingly infinite black hole of ignorance. It happened on unit – 4. Yes, poor old, abused unit – 4. It continuously suffered the wrath of my focused ability to inflict operations on it.

It was late autumn in 1978, and the elevated New Mexico desert surrounding Four Corners had a visceral chill that migrated straight to your bones. In the control room, I was suffering through another of many non-ending graveyard shifts. This, of course, was not unusual. Night shifts were always a killer. At about 3:40 A.M., I received an alarm for low oil temperature on the main turbine. I was at 760 MW gross. I was producing 760 million watts or over 1 million horsepower from the turbine and generator.

Four Corners is at or near 5000' elevation. It may be in New Mexico, but it is in far northern New Mexico, and it is no stranger to freezing conditions in the winter. Morgan Lake, though quite warm in the summer, cooled substantially in fall and winter. Since the lake water ultimately supplied all the plant cooling systems, there was an abundance of cooling capacity after the lake cooled for the winter.

The turbine bearing oil temperature low alarm sounded at 110° Fahrenheit. I looked at the trend chart and could see it was slowly dropping. Obviously, something was wonky on the temperature control system. The turbine lubricating oil was supposed to be 115° F to 120° F when the turbine was online. My racing days left me with an understanding that overheated lubricating oil was bad, very bad. I never considered cold oil as being a problem. What I didn't realize was cold oil was a far more serious issue than warm oil on a massive turbine like this one.

25 psig of lubricating oil pressure is pumped into the gap between the stationary bearing surfaces and the shaft rotating at 3600 RPM. Even though the turbine shaft is shiny and smooth, it still motivates or moves the oil through the bearing. As the viscosity of the oil increases, the pumping action increases, changing the dynamics inside the bearings. If the viscosity increases too much due to the oil being too cold, a condition known as "oil whip" occurs.

Oil whip causes the turbine shaft to vibrate aggressively. It is a non-synchronous vibration which means that out of 11 bearings on the turbine rotor, all of them are vibrating independently of the others. This gets messy, incredibly messy. I had no idea just how messy…

Watching the oil temperature decrease did not cause any alarm or reflective pause within me. Something was obviously wrong, but it probably wasn't serious because the oil was *just getting cooler.* In my mind, with my limited experience and understanding, this was the least serious direction for failure. If it were getting warmer, I would have been alarmed enough to call for immediate help from someone. Cold oil? Not so much. I casually paged my Auxiliary Operator and told him to check the main turbine lube oil coolers as my oil temperature decreased. There was no urgency or alarm in my voice or demeanor.

The turbine lube oil coolers are located inside the large main turbine lube oil reservoir. This was a huge square tank with a 12' steel ladder on the side so the operator could climb to inspect the three large, electric-driven oil pumps and the vapor extractor. The top of the coolers is accessed from the top of the reservoir. The lube oil temperature control valve was pneumatically actuated.

Apparently, the air supply line to the control valve had come loose, and the approximately 15" cooling water valve failed in the open position. This caused excessive cooling water to flow through the coolers. My Auxiliary Operator looked the situation over and, for no apparent reason, cracked-open the bypass valve to put MORE cooling water through the coolers. This act of total ignorance on his part probably saved my job.

The General Electric operating manuals strongly warn against increasing the turbine speed over 3000 RPM until the oil temperature is above 100° F MINIMUM. *I mean, what do they know? They just designed and built the unit.* Unfortunately, somewhere around 100°, all hell broke loose. The huge, cross-compound steam turbine producing over a million horsepower went into high vibration. How high? *Off the charts high.* The turbine immediately tripped due to the dangerously high vibration and rolled down to a stop in about 3 minutes. This is significant. Normally, these massive turbines would take over an hour and a half to coast down due to the amount of weight and inertia in the shafts.

There was significant damage to the turbine. If I were a fighter pilot, I would have now been considered an ace had I downed as many enemy aircraft as the number of serious failures I inflicted on the units at Four Corners.

Oddly, I was not reprimanded in writing for my failure. The accident analysis revealed the air supply line to the turbine lube oil cooler was fractured, bleeding the air off the valve and rendering it uncontrollable. My Auxiliary Operator took far more heat than I did because he did the absolute wrong thing by opening the bypass to put even **MORE** water through the cooler.

Management questioned me at length and apparently was satisfied that had he asked me for direction, I would have told him to do the right thing. In my heart, I knew if he had been working for a decent control room operator, he might have been told to do this while he was contacted to check the oil coolers. Once again, I dodged a HUGE bullet and walked away penalty-free. APS (and poor old unit – 4) again paid the price.

During this time-period, something spiritual was awakening inside me. While we never attended Church the entire time we lived in Farmington, something was moving inside me. I couldn't put my finger on it. Something was just different inside me. I seemed to be more aware of something bigger than me. Ever since my experience at the pumphouse, I have seen things differently.

Besides what happened at the pumphouse, I was marveling that I had lost all desire to drink alcohol. I was certainly consuming an inordinate amount of apple juice, but in one moment, I lost all desire to drink alcohol. Things were changing inside me. Something major took place place in my life. I turned a spiritual corner and was now going in a completely different direction.

I also knew that I MUST get out of Four Corners. I began to get antsy about the resume' I sent to Laramie River Station. This feeling of having to get away was the *exact* same feeling I had before we left Rock Springs. I just knew I had to get out. I felt like my life depended on it.

After several weeks, I could not take the suspense, so I called Laramie River Station to see what was happening. Unfortunately, I was told it was too early. They were still collecting resumes and hadn't even hired the Operations Manager yet. Ugh! How was I supposed to leave Four Corners with them dragging their feet? *After all, they were building this plant for me, right?*

~7~

Laramie River Station

Several weeks later, I received a call from Mr. Orville (Bert) Donovan of Basin Electric Power Cooperative. This was the company building and operating the Laramie River Station. It was about 11:00 A.M, and I was home because I had not left for the afternoon shift at the plant.

I was sitting with Vangie in the front room, playing with Brandi on the floor. I jumped up and answered the phone when it rang. We had not made any friends in Farmington other than Harley and Loren Kelly, and since stealing the instruments for Harley, we were on the outs. The only time the phone ever rang was when the plant called with an overtime request or the rare occasion that one of our folks called.

"Hello." I figured the plant wanted me to come in early to fill in for someone. However, it was an unrecognized man's voice.

"Could I speak to Mark Gregg, please?"

"Speaking."

"Mr. Gregg, my name is Bert Donovan. I am the Operations Supervisor at Laramie River Station, and I am reviewing your resume." He paused. "Do you have a few minutes to answer some questions about your control room operator application?" He had a direct, commanding voice.

"I have as much time as you need. I am very interested in your plant." I was working hard to contain my excitement.

"I noticed you started at Jim Bridger Plant before going to Four Corners. Did you know a Shift Supervisor named Marvin Riddle?" His voice inflection indicated he was leading me somewhere.

"Of course!" I answered enthusiastically. "He helped train me, and I worked for him as a laborer." I paused and took the bait. "Do you know Marv?"

"As a matter of fact, I do. I just hired him as a Shift Supervisor to help with the start-up." He seemed very pleased with himself as he continued. "Marvin is helping sort through the applications for Control Room Operator, and he pulled yours out of the stack."

"That's fantastic!" I was now elated and relieved, and I couldn't possibly hide it as I gushed, "I am really glad to hear it because I want to do a new unit startup more than you could ever know."

Bert approvingly asked, "Would you be willing to come to Wheatland, Wyoming and interview in person?"

I felt the weight of the world leaving my shoulders. It was as if God himself were talking to me at this moment.

"You name the time, and I will use some vacation and come out." I could hardly contain myself now. It was one of those key moments in life when, deep inside, you knew this was meant to be.

I hung-up the phone and immediately looked at Vangie, barely containing my excitement and said, "That was Laramie River Station in Wheatland, Wyoming. They are building a new, 3 unit plant and want me to interview for Control Room Operator.

"Wyoming? *Again?*" She looked irritated as she continued. "You were super-excited about getting out of Wyoming 18 months ago; why so excited to go back now?"

"It ISN'T Rock Springs! It is on the opposite side of the state. It is only a couple of hours from Denver. It is a brand-new plant that I would be starting up!"

"Save the sales pitch!" She retorted quickly. "I am fine with going to see Wheatland. Please just keep it honest here. *YOU* want to go to a new power plant. It has nothing to do with a newer, nicer area to live in or anything else. You just want to go to a new power plant."

Vangie certainly had a way of ALWAYS bringing things to the most common denominator. She was not loving Farmington, but she knew this entire desire to move was based on nothing but my failures at Four Corners and not necessarily to better our family's living situation.

Vangie and I discussed the possibility of moving for the next few weeks. She was reticent to say much because she was concerned about moving to another "boom town" in Wyoming.

I couldn't blame her after our experience in Rock Springs. The only thing that made it easier for her to consider going back to Wyoming was Farmington wasn't a very nice place to live and had many problems caused by high levels of substance abuse. As for me, I could not see *ANYTHING* except getting away from Four Corners, which is odd considering the very job I considered the pinnacle of life was already mine. It seems that major accomplishments in life are, sometimes, bitter-sweet.

We chose to drive to Wheatland. It was a chance to get away from Farmington, and we stopped and spent the evening with Gloria and Patrick, Vangie's sister and husband. It was a nice visit.

We stopped for gas in Cheyenne, which is directly across the Colorado border. It appeared to be an older town, and it seemed odd that it was right on the southern border of the state and yet still the capital. I always thought capitals were supposed to be more centrally located in a state. This is not the case in Wyoming.

We were surprised at just how small the capital of Wyoming appeared. The population of Cheyenne was only 45,000 people. Not enough to even be considered a city. The population of the *entire state* of Wyoming in 1978 was about 430,000 people. There were more people in Denver than in the entire state of Wyoming.

There are windsocks at various points on I-25 going north from Cheyenne. Time would reveal to us that the wind rarely ceased in that area. The windsocks warned truckers that crosswinds could be, and frequently were deadly. Indeed, the little Toyota Chinook camper was severely buffeted by heavy crosswinds all the way to Wheatland, 70 miles to the north.

I was getting concerned about Vangie as the wind took siege on the little Toyota camper. She HATED the wind. She had always told me this. I was freaking out because I did not want her to sour on Wheatland before we even saw the town. *There was plenty of time for this later.*

As we exited I-25 into Wheatland, Black Mountain Village could be seen on the interstate's left side. What do you do if you are hosting up to 10,000 construction workers in a town of 2,000 people? You build a massive trailer park to house the influx of people. Black Mountain Village was the epitome of an absolute massive trailer park.

Platte County, Wyoming, with Wheatland being the county seat, had a spot in the Guinness Book of World Records for the most churches per capita in the United States. No, it wasn't the Bible Belt. It was just a lot of very independent people who simply split off and started their own Church every time there was a major disagreement amongst a congregation. There was a Church on almost every corner.

Our drive through the small, dusty, wind-blown hamlet revealed one stoplight. It was an easy town to navigate. There was not much to it. It appeared that 9th Street was the main street. The downtown businesses were a perfect setting for a 1940s movie.

The Platte County Courthouse on 9th Street was probably built in the early 1900's. The far end of 9th Street had a large, aging mill of some sort. I thought it was a flour factory because there was white dust coated around the doors, windows, and every other opening. With a name like Wheatland, a flour mill seemed appropriate. I later found out they crushed and dyed decorative rock for aquariums or other uses. It had nothing to do with wheat or flour.

After the quick jaunt down the main street in town, we circled back and pulled into the Taco Johns drive-thru restaurant and had a taco. Across the street was a mini-mart. It seemed to be the hub of the entire town. The traffic in and out of this convenience store and gas station was remarkable… Mostly pickups and teenagers, but continuous. The town was old, forgettable, and a bit depressing.

"Not much here," Vangie stated drolly, void of emotion.

"It is probably a nice place to raise kids." I was grasping for anything positive.

"REALLY?" She was borderline irritated. "Don't pull your salesman crap on me. It is an old, wind-blown town with one stoplight. What part of this makes it a good town to raise kids?"

"At least give it a chance." I felt my temper rising, but I did NOT want a fight right now. I just wanted to get my interview out of the way.

We found the city park on the southeast side of town. It was a beautiful oasis in the midst of windblown hell. This park was undoubtedly the nicest public area in town. It was large, had plenty of trees and a well-groomed, emerald green lawn, and playground equipment that appeared well maintained. It even had a small, public campground adjoining it. I needed even a small victory. This would have to be it for now. I decided we would stay the night there.

We drove to the partially constructed plant, and Vangie let me out. She was going back to the park and play with Brandi. I told her to come back in a couple of hours. If I got done with the interview earlier, I would simply start walking to town. She then surprised me as only she could.

She hugged me as I got out of the vehicle and whispered in my ear, "Good luck! I know you will do well. I love you!" She was so sincere and loving when she wanted to be. This was one of those moments. It raised my spirits exponentially. I had yet to learn that she just wanted honesty from me. She did not like it when I would go into salesman mode and try to convince her of something when I was really saying something else. She knew very well it didn't matter what the town looked like… I was fixed on getting that job. Nothing else mattered. She was a smart, mature girl. Far smarter and more mature than me.

I met Bert Donovan at an old farmhouse temporarily being used as the operations office. Construction was not finished on the massive admin building attached to the plant.

Rather than interview me in the office, we jumped into his company pickup and started driving. Bert was distinguished, knowledgeable, and appeared to be a hard-ass. He looked to be in his early 40s and was the Operations Supervisor at a large, lignite-fired plant in North Dakota before being hired here.

Bert's personality and demeanor was total authoritarian and frankly… He intimidated the hell out of me. I would later come to realize that there was only one person at that entire plant that loved power plants as much as I did. It was Bert Donovan. Regardless of the intimidation I felt, we seemed to hit it off.

We drove slowly around the plant site abuzz with thousands of construction workers. There wasn't much to see inside the plant yet due to the early stages of construction, so the entire interview was conducted in his pickup as we toured the massive plant site.

The interview continued casually, and there were no "hard" questions until he abruptly stopped the truck by the unit – 1 cooling tower basin. He looked at me, cleared his throat and said, "Tell me the key to being a control room operator at a plant like this." His intense stare made me uneasy.

I thought about it for several seconds and then silently choked because I didn't have a good answer. I finally stammered, "You have to bird-dog your Auxiliary Operators..." I trailed-off.

Immediately after saying this, I felt like a total, complete idiot. Where did that even come from? Why would I say something this utterly stupid? I was panicking. I could tell that he let me stew for a few moments before helping me out.

"The control room operator is responsible for the safety and well-being of every individual on the plant site when the unit is operating." As soon as he said this, he put the truck into gear and headed back to the farmhouse. I was sick to my stomach. How could I not say this or something else, at least in the realm of sensibility? Instead, I dropped the ball and said something completely ridiculous.

After arriving back at the farmhouse, he promptly ended the interview with, "We will let you know in a few weeks. We have several more interviews to conduct." I felt like I hit a brick wall. I thanked him for the interview, shook his hand, and started walking back towards town on the plant road.

I was walking westward to get back to the main highway and town. In the distance was the stately Medicine Bow Mountain range. The sky was a mesmerizing azure hue smattered with expansive, billowy white clouds flirting with Laramie Peak, the tallest mountain in the Medicine Bow range.

My stress level evaporated as I stared at a celestial portrait that only God could paint. The colors were more vivid and intense than my finite mind could grasp. As I stared reverently into the sky, absorbing the magnificent visual symphony of the clouds and the mountains, I was completely enveloped in an inexplicable calm, not of my own making. I quietly sequenced from fretting and anxiety to complete, unexplainable peace.

I walked about a mile before Vangie arrived to pick me up. Brandi was asleep in the back, and Vangie looked relaxed. We talked about Wheatland and the interview a bit. I was oddly euphoric. Due to the drive from Denver to Wheatland and then the interview, I realized I was also tired. We stayed the night in Wheatland and then left the next morning, returning to Farmington.

~7~

Farewell Debacle at Four Corners

Several weeks passed after my interview at Laramie River Station. I was becoming disheartened at the lack of a phone call. I finally couldn't wait any longer and called Bert Donovan, only to be told there were construction delays at the plant, pushing back the hiring process.

This news threw me into a tailspin. I knew that if they interviewed enough candidates, they would unquestionably find better, more experienced operators than me. I had less than three years of total experience. Dealing with extreme self-doubt and concern, I was stuck at Four Corners with my horrible reputation; I began sending my resume' to other plants. Unfortunately, no one was beating down the door to hire me.

At a dead crawl, autumn sequenced into winter 1978. Indeed, this winter was shaping up to be a bad one. The plant wasn't to be spared the season's rath nor the incompetence of a particular operator desperate to leave the area.

The early winter months became quite intense at the Four Corners Plant. The plant demineralizer systems were out of service due to serious maintenance issues. We were running out of demineralized water. This situation is extremely serious because you can't run a plant without abundant, high-purity, demineralized water.

During this time period, the call finally came in from Bert Donovan. He offered me a Control Room Operator position at the Laramie River

Station. The pay was almost $2.00 an hour less than I was making at Four Corners, but this did not faze me. I wholeheartedly accepted and thanked him profusely for the offer. He said the starting date for the new Control Room Operators was Monday, February 12th, 1979. To say I was elated, overjoyed, and thankful is a gross understatement. I could barely contain my joy and was virtually giddy at the acceptance of the job.

The spiritual awakening that I was feeling caused me to drop to my knees and thank God for the job offer. I was emotional as I prayed. Knowing I had an "out" from Four Corners was such a stress release. I gave my two-week resignation notice to APS the week after Christmas 1978. It was gladly received. Dicky Mundt was the happiest I had seen him in months. For the first time ever, he treated me like a human for almost a week.

The second and final week of my two-week notice at Four Corners was a graveyard shift. I was more exhausted than usual due to packing and making moving preparations. It was bitterly cold outside, and a winter storm was forecast for the area.

Arriving at the plant that night revealed only two units running. Unit – 3 and Unit – 4. This was not a good thing. When the weather gets this cold, the plants are required for the grid, and it is never good to be offline in cold weather because it is very difficult to keep instrument lines, controllers, and other critical devices from freezing.

I found out at shift turnover that unit – 1 had a boiler tube leak, and unit – 2 had a fan problem. Unit – 3 and four were running, and unit – 5 also had a boiler tube leak.

I recorded my initial set of required hourly data. I am certain this was strictly to force us, the operators, to look at our units during a shift.

I recorded my condensate storage tank level at 3'. This was almost completely empty. It was a half-million-gallon tank and virtually no demineralized water was left in it. APS was continuously purchasing tank trucks of demineralized water from the San Juan Power Plant about 25 miles away, but it didn't last long.

Unit – 4 was maxed out at 750 MW net and appeared to be running well despite the cold weather. I settled in for a grueling night of trying to remain awake. I HATED GRAVEYARD SHIFTS! One nice thing about going to Laramie River Station was the fact that we would be on the day shift for several months during the training period.

About two hours into the shift, I sat at the control operator's desk and drifted to sleep. I was startled by the telephone ringing on my desk. It was Teddy Smallgorge from the unit – 3 control room.

"Dis-is-Teddy." He seemed to struggle harder with English than most of the Navajo there. "I-running-out-water. You-transfer-some-to-me?"

"Just a minute, and I will see what I have." I was trying to sound like I was awake and cognizant, but the truth is his call woke me, and I was disheveled.

I set the phone down and looked on the back panel at my condensate storage tank level gage. It was 32+ feet. This was all the way full and then some. It seemed surreal to me that it could be this full because when I arrived at the plant a couple of hours earlier, it was almost empty. There was no possible way they could have processed enough trucks even to come close to filling this massive 500,000-gallon demineralized water tank.

I wasn't sure what was going on, but I picked the phone back up and said, "Teddy, I have enough water to transfer some to you. I will get my Auxiliary Operator to line it up."

"Thank-you. I-haffa-go-cuz-of-alarms." Teddy abruptly hung up the phone.

I called my Auxiliary Operator and told him to line up and start a condensate transfer to unit − 3. I then sat back down satisfied that I responded properly. It was only a few minutes before I drifted off to sleep again when a critical alarm sounded. The critical alarms would flash with a red background. I looked up, and the alarm window read: "LOW CONDENSER VACUUM".

The steam turbine MUST exhaust into a vacuum for efficiency and safety. If the pressure in the condenser gets more than 7" absolute (less than about 23" of vacuum), the turbine trips to protect the long, low-pressure section blading from windage and high temperatures.

My heart leaped into overdrive as I jumped up to the control board. Both vacuum pumps were running. I knew that if the turbine gland steam seal system malfunctioned, it could pull air across the shaft and reduce vacuum. At this same moment, I heard what sounded like Teddy Smallgorge hollering over the paging system, "Unit − 3, trip! Unit − 3 trip!

I turned to look at the turbine steam seal pressure, and there was a loud **BLAM!!!** My steam turbine tripped. This tripped the boiler (as it was supposed to), and the two 16,500 HP boiler feed pump turbines tripped. You could hear them winding down in the background. Alarms were popping up quicker than I could process them. Dicky and Rick Kiering ran out of their office and into the control room. Dicky was the first to speak (yell).

"WHAT THE HELL HAPPENED!" He violently pushed me aside from the board to see what he could see. I was almost knocked off my feet as he forced himself in front of me.

"I got a low vacuum alarm, and the unit tripped almost instantly." I tried to be as professional as possible despite being totally pissed at how I was just manhandled.

"WHAT'S YOUR CONDENSATE STORAGE TANK LEVEL?" He whipped around to the backboard, looking at the level gage for the condensate storage tank.

As he looked at the level instrumentation, I said, "My condensate storage tank was topped off, so I transferred some water to unit – 3 because his storage tank was empty." I was trying to be proactive with his investigation.

"I AM CERTAIN YOUR TANK IS *$#@ing EMPTY!" He screamed at the top of his lungs. *"WHO TOLD YOU TO TRANSFER WATER TO THE OTHER SIDE?"* Dicky looked demonic, and his voice had jumped an octave.

"No one." I was numb and didn't care that he was screaming. I was just done as I finished with, "Teddy Smallgorge called and said he was running out of water. My tank was completely full, so I sent him some."

"YOU ARE A *$#@ing IDIOT!" He was screaming even louder now and had fire in his eyes. *"YOUR CONDENSATE STORAGE TANK LEVEL IS A PRESSURE TRANSMITTER THAT USES THE HEAD PRESSURE IN THE TANK AND CONVERTS IT TO READ LEVEL. IT OBVIOUSLY FROZE AND IS GIVING YOU A FALSE INDICATION!"*

I realized he was right. There is no way my tank could have increased from empty to full in two hours. I knew this when I looked at it earlier, but I was so tired I just took it for granted and moved on.

It took the rest of the morning to secure the unit. Neither unit – 3 nor unit – 4 could restart because we had no water. Everyone in the plant was freaking out because it was so cold that things were already freezing. At about 6:00 that morning, Dicky called me into his office. He had an intense and demented look on his ugly jack-o-lantern mug.

"The best thing you could do is leave this morning and not *EVER* come back." He looked pissed enough that I didn't want to challenge him. "You will be paid through this morning when your final check is mailed to you." He shook his head before continuing. "You are leaving us in an amazing mess here. You should have never been given the Control Room Operator position..." His voice trailed off. "Hell, *you should have never been hired!"*

I was dead tired, wrung out, and had enough of his crap. I spent weeks being bruised, bullied and treated worse than a criminal. I decided that I wouldn't leave without telling him how I really felt.

"I did the best I could considering the crappy training I received and the lousy way I was treated."

The color instantly drained from his face, and his expression turned to pure violence. He quickly jumped up from his desk, and I thought he would draw back and hit me. Instead, he immediately bounced around his desk, threw open the door, and seethed with clinched teeth, "Get the *$#@ out and don't ever darken the door of this plant again." I left his office with my head down, justifiably feeling terrible about myself. I didn't want to leave the plant this way. Who would?

Anyway, it was over, and I was now free to start a new life elsewhere and do things right this time. I had every intention of doing just that. I wanted to be the best control room operator they had at Laramie River Station. I needed to put this chapter of my life as far behind me as possible.

We only attended Church twice in Rock Springs, Wyoming, and never attended Church the entire time we lived in Farmington. Despite this, I was supernaturally cured of my alcohol addiction. I didn't know where it was found in the Bible then, but I couldn't get out of my mind the scripture that said, *"Therefore, if anyone is in Christ, the new creation has come: The old has gone, the new is here!"*

Later in my life, I learned this was found in 2nd Corinthians, Chapter - 5, Verse – 17. The old me died in Farmington. That evening at the river pumphouse, I faced death. It doesn't matter what anyone thinks when they read about it. My decision to follow Christ that evening changed my life forever. The old died, and the new started that very night. Church had nothing to do with it. We never attended any Church whatsoever in Farmington.

I was supernaturally touched by the God of creation, and we were now embarking on a brand new, amazing path in life. One that would find us experiencing many *documented* miracles that changed our lives and the lives of people around us. Our lives would never be the same after this.